MW01631098

ORIGINAL

FERRARI V8

Other titles available in the *Original* series are:

Original AC Ace & Cobra
by Rinsey Mills
Original Aston Martin DB4/5/6
by Robert Edwards
Original Austin Seven
by Rinsey Mills
Original Austin-Healey (100 & 3000)
by Anders Ditlev Clausager
Original Citroën DS
by John Reynolds with Jan de Lange
Original Jaguar XK
by Philip Porter
Original Jaguar E-Type
by Philip Porter
Original Jaguar Mark I/II
by Nigel Thorley
Original Land-Rover Series I
by James Taylor
Original Mercedes SL
by Laurence Meredith
Original MG T Series
by Anders Ditlev Clausager
Original MGA
by Anders Ditlev Clausager
Original MGB
by Anders Ditlev Clausager
Original Mini Cooper and Cooper S
by John Parnell
Original Morgan
by John Worrall and Liz Turner
Original Morris Minor
by Ray Newell
Original Porsche 356
by Laurence Meredith
Original Porsche 911
by Peter Morgan
Original Sprite & Midget
by Terry Horler
Original Triumph TR
by Bill Piggott
Original Vincent
by J. Bickerstaff
Original VW Beetle
by Laurence Meredith
Original VW Bus
by Laurence Meredith

ORIGINAL FERRARI V8

by Keith Bluemel

Photography by Paul Debois, Dieter Rebmann and James Mann

Edited by Mark Hughes

On the front cover: The best-selling Ferrari ever, and to many eyes, also the best-looking of all the V8-powered cars—the 328 series of 1985–89 hit new heights of popularity with 1334 GTB and 6068 GTS models built.

On the half-title page: Not too different from a 308 GTB at a glance, but this is the wonderful 288 GTO. Twin-turbo V8 engine developing 400bhp gave top speed of 189.6mph (305kph) for this exclusive machine—only 272 were built.

On the title page: Bertone-designed 308 GT4—the first production Ferrari with the V8 engine—provided superb packaging by combining mid-engined layout with 2+2 seating, but it was not a great success with only 2826 built between 1974–80. Thereafter the 2+2 configuration continued for the similarily under-rated Mondial series, designed, like all subsequent V8-powered Ferraris, by Pininfarina.

On the back cover: F40 was comfortably the fastest of the V8-powered Ferraris, and also the fastest road car in the world during its 1987–92 production period. Purposeful looks are very different from those of 288 GTO, but F40 evolved directly from this model, with twin-turbo power output raised to 478bhp to give a top speed of 201.3mph (323kph). The factory has been guarded about stating total production, but it can be confirmed as 1311.

This edition first published in 1997 by Motorbooks International, an imprint of MBI Publishing Company, Galtier Plaza, Suite 200, 380 Jackson Street, St. Paul, MN 55101-3885 USA

Library of Congress Cataloging-in-Publication Data available
ISBN 1-870979-78-8

Type and design by Chris Fayers & Sarah Ward
Printed in China

CONTENTS

INTRODUCTION

There are purists who take the view that a 'true' Ferrari must have a V12 engine at the front, or, to coin a phrase attributed to Enzo Ferrari, with the horse pulling the cart. Some take it even further by interpreting Fiat's 1969 takeover of the road car business as a cut-off point for a 'true' Ferrari.

The facts of the matter are that Ferrari, even prior to 1969, produced a wide variety of engine configurations for racing machinery – there were very successful four-cylinder racing Ferraris in the 1950s. Although the V12 is synonymous with the Ferrari name, the other configurations shared designers, engineers, mechanics, foundry and machine shops, so there is no logical basis for this stance. In fact since 1974, when the first V8-engined model, the 308 GT4, went into production, more Ferraris have been produced with V8s than any other engine layout in the company's history, and even today V8s remain the backbone of the production car range in terms of volume sales.

My task in unravelling the specification evolution of the V8 models for this book, the first Ferrari title in the *Original* series, began with background research from other books and swiftly moved on to factory-produced owner's handbooks, parts manuals and workshop manuals, careful study of these latter sources providing invaluable detail information and explanations of how mechanical features fitted together and operated. Thank you especially to Ferrari SpA.

On a personal level, the entire exercise was made much easier due to the help afforded by Jacques Swaters of Garage Francorchamps, who kindly made available to me, as a friend, the incomparable library of factory literature in his FF Galleria in Brussels, and also eased the passage in obtaining information from the factory. I would go as far as to say that the task would have been almost insurmountable without his kindness and assistance. Similarly, thanks are due to his staff in the persons of Bernard Dubois, Patrick Pochez and Roberto Bernardi, who gave their time to answer a multitude of questions and check details for me.

On my side of the English Channel, Peter Whittle, Steve Lay and Tim Bates of Ferrari UK were also very helpful in sourcing elusive information over a considerable period of time, and I thank them for their time, effort and patience. Another who assisted greatly was Tony Willis of Maranello Sales Ltd, who kindly gave me free rein on numerous occasions to wander his workshops, poring over cars to check and note details, and who also afforded help on the photographic side, as did Mike Wheeler of Talacrest Ltd.

'Disegno di Pininfarina': this badge on rear flanks is a common link between all V8-powered models except the first, the 308 GT4, which was designed by Bertone. Turin-based Pininfarina has been Ferrari's favoured designer ever since the mid-1950s.

For providing information, thanks must also go to a long-standing friend in Japan, Michitake Isobe, who checked Japanese market variations and sent reams of facsimile messages with information and encouragement. On a practical level, my thanks go to Denny Schue, Ross Gibson, Jamie White, Les Duplock and, in particular, his wife June, whose deft fingers on the word processor translated my scribble into a legible form in record time to meet the deadline.

Many owners have allowed their cars to be specially photographed for this book, primarily by Paul Debois in the UK, Dieter Rebmann in Germany and James Mann in the US. Those who should be singled out are Steve Turner (308 GT4), John Bicourt (308 GTS US), Rick de Simone of Algar Enterprises (308 GTSi), Terry Johnson (308 GTBi QV), Allan Pepper (Mondial 8), Bill Doran (Mondial QV Cabriolet), Richard Browning (Mondial 3.2), Joe Stampone (348 Serie Speciale), Archer MacLean (288 GTO) and Richard Koppelman of Miller Motorcars (various details). Peter Everingham of the Ferrari Owners Club (UK) and Wendy Eberle of the Ferrari Club of America helped to locate cars. Some photos of my own are included, and others have been supplied by Alessandro Giudice, Peter Braun, Michitake Isobe, Ira Schwartz and Neill Bruce.

Without the help of all of these allies, together with encouragement from many others, I could not have written this book, and I thank them all sincerely and unreservedly.

Keith Bluemel
February 1997

V8 FERRARIS PAST & PRESENT

Gorgeous from any angle, lines of mid-engined V6 Dino 246 GT – immediate ancestor of V8-powered cars covered in this book – were so finely sculpted by Pininfarina.

The roots of eight-cylinder Ferrari engines go back even further than the marque itself. When, in 1939, Enzo Ferrari terminated his agreement with Alfa Romeo to run its racing team under his Scuderia Ferrari banner, one of the severance terms was that he could not construct a car bearing his name for a minimum period of four years. To circumnavigate this contractual obligation, he started racing car manufacture under the umbrella of his machine tool company, Auto Avio Costruzioni, and in 1940 he produced his first two cars.

These machines carried only a single badge on the nose above the radiator grille. It featured a *Cavallino Rampante* – 'Prancing Horse' – and the figures 815. Thus the first 'Ferrari' was born, the 8 referring to the number of cylinders and the 15 to the 1500cc engine size. Such juxtaposition of figures in a model title, to indicate number of cylinders and capacity, was to become a periodic feature on Ferraris, particularly for V6 and V8 models. Incidentally, Ferrari's other – and historically more usual – system of three-figure designation indicates the cubic capacity of one cylinder.

The 815 relied heavily on Fiat components in its construction. The straight-eight engine was created by mating two de-stroked Fiat 1100C four-cylinder blocks, while the chassis was a modified Fiat 508C unit with the brakes, steering, suspension and transmission taken from the same model. The body was an open two-seater design by Carrozzeria Touring of Milan, constructed in light aluminium to that company's patented *superleggera* concept. Of the two examples built, one is believed to have been destroyed while the other, chassis number 021, is owned by an Italian collector.

In the latter part of 1940 a specification was drawn up for an 815B model, although, as far as is known, it never went further than a proposal. In 1941 a mechanical specification was produced for an 811 model (8 cylinders, 1100cc), with Zagato producing body design drawings for this model. However, the war in Europe was becoming more intense and the output of Auto Avio Costruzioni was to be confined to small aero engines and machine tools for the duration of the conflict.

When the first car appeared after the war, in 1947, it was able to carry a Ferrari badge because the Alfa Romeo clauses had expired. This model was the 125S, powered by a newly designed V12 engine. Eight-cylinder credentials, however, are firmly established in Ferrari's history, and such engines have appeared intermittently among the many engine configurations produced by the company since its inception.

During the early 1950s Ferrari built V12s, straight-sixes and straight-fours for its sports racing models, V12s and straight-fours for the single-seaters, and V12s only for the road cars. An eight-cylinder engine did not appear in the line-up until mid-1955, when Ferrari 'inherited' the Lancia D50 Formula 1 cars, which were raced in Grands Prix as Lancia-Ferraris for the rest of that season and as Ferrari-Lancias during 1956, when Fangio won the World Championship for the team.

By 1956, Ferrari had developed the Lancia 90° V8 to raise power output from 250bhp to 265bhp. Increased cylinder bore and reduced stroke gave a capacity 2486cc, against the original engine's 2488cc, and there were revisions to the timing system and a redesigned crankshaft. The engine was further developed for the 801 model of 1957, but despite an additional 20bhp these cars were no match for the Maserati 250Fs and Vanwalls, ending that season without a single victory.

The 1958 season saw a switch to a V6 engine for the 246 Dino Formula 1 car, with far greater success – Mike Hawthorn won the World Championship after a season-long battle with Stirling Moss. This V6 engine took the name 'Dino' from Enzo Ferrari's late son, who had been working on the project with Vittorio Jano prior to his premature death in 1956, aged only 24. The basic design was to become the cornerstone for subsequent V6 models – and for the V8 road cars covered in this book.

The Formula 1 cars, rear-engined from the imposition of a 1.5-litre limit in 1961, used V6 engines until the end of 1963. For 1964 a new V8 engine, as well as a flat-12, powered the cars in which John Surtees won the World Championship. As with all subsequent Ferrari V8 engines, the vee angle was 90°.

On the sports racing front, meanwhile, several cars had used V8 engines carrying the Dino name. The first was the type 298S V8 of 1957 with a twin overhead camshaft engine of 3 litres, while the 248 GT of 1961

Stages in V6/V8 lineage, part one: 1940 Auto Avio Costruzioni 815 model (top left) used 1500cc straight-eight engine adapted from two four-cylinder Fiat units; V6-powered 246 Dino (top right) took Mike Hawthorn to 1958 World Championship title; 1500cc V8 F1 engine of 1964 (above left), as used by John Surtees to win that year's World Championship; Dino with fuel-injected 2.4-litre V6 engine (above right) won Tasman titles for Chris Amon (1969) and Graeme Lawrence (1970).

Stages in V6/V8 lineage, part two: elegant 206S of 1966 (lower left and lower right), looking rather like a scaled-down 330 P3/4 sports racer, reveals similarities in overall shape to later road-going Dinos, particularly in front wing lines and radiator intake; Pininfarina's first Dino offering (bottom left), displayed at 1965 Paris salon, predicted styling of production model except for headlight arrangement; this design was followed by Pininfarina's radical winged prototype (bottom right), built on a competition 206S chassis.

and the 268S of 1962 both used single overhead camshaft engines. During 1961 the factory also ran a 246S V6 engine, which continued into 1962, when the 196S V6 was also introduced. The former was basically a modified version of the 246 Dino Formula 1 engine, while the latter had a single overhead camshaft per bank of cylinders. The V6 engines seemed to produce better results than their V8 cousins, with Ludovico Scarfiotti winning the 1962 European Mountain Championship in a 196SP. The 246SP took overall victory in the demanding Targa Florio in 1961 and 1962, and also won the Nürburgring 1000kms in 1962.

After the 1964 World Championship victory, there would be no place for a V8 engine in Ferrari's plans for another decade. However, the Dino V6 engine layout was resurrected in 1965, when the 166P sports racing model was introduced. This 1.6-litre engine had twin overhead camshafts per bank, a 65° vee angle, and ran on triple twin-choke Weber carburettors. In mid-season this car was fitted with a 2-litre version of the engine to contest the European Mountain Championship once again, in the hands of Scarfiotti as in 1962. Despite having missed the first two rounds, the combination was dominant in the remaining events and the title went to Ferrari. A single-seater variant with a 2.4-litre V6 was developed late in 1965 with a view to contesting that winter's Tasman series, held in Australia and New Zealand, but this plan evaporated when the chosen driver, John Surtees, was injured in a CanAm accident.

In 1966 the 206S Dino sports racing model was presented. An elegant little jewel, it looked like a scaled-down 330P3/4 and was similarly produced in open and coupé forms. These cars were campaigned in international events by the factory and private teams until 1970, and a single-seater was developed in both Formula 2 and Tasman forms. The record book shows that the Formula 2 version won the South American Temporada series for Andrea de Adamich (1968), while the Tasman car won that series with Chris Amon (1969) and Graeme Lawrence (1970).

Thus far all of Ferrari's V8 and V6 engines had been for competition use. Not until the announcement of new Formula 2 regulations, to take effect in 1967, did any cross-breeding with road cars take place. These

Timelessly elegant Dino 246 GT, considered by many to be one of Pininfarina's finest masterpieces. One can see why Bertone-designed 308 GT4 found it such a hard act to follow.

revised rules dictated that Formula 2 cars used an engine block of production car origin, with at least 500 cars built in a 12-month period. This production level was beyond Ferrari's capability (the company was building around 700 V12-engined cars a year at that time), so the solution was a venture with Fiat whereby a Ferrari-designed V6 with cast iron block would go into a new Fiat sports car.

The Fiat Dino was presented to the public at the 1966 Turin Salon in two versions, both with a 2-litre V6 engine, in-line gearbox and conventional rigid rear axle. The first was a 2+2 coupé designed by Bertone, the second a beautiful two-seater spider by Pininfarina that echoed the general lines of a mid-engined Dino prototype exhibited by this designer at the 1965 Paris Salon.

This 1965 design exercise pointed the way for a new series of 'compact' mid-engined Ferrari road cars. A second prototype was shown on the Pininfarina stand at the 1966 Turin Salon, still with a longitudinal mid-engined configuration, but the general body lines had altered. They had been developed into a shape very close to what would become the Ferrari-built Dino 206 GT road car, presented in its definitive form – with transverse engine and unitary transmission – at the 1967 Turin Salon.

Another Pininfarina prototype was built in 1967 and exhibited at the Frankfurt Salon. Described as a 'Dino Berlinetta Prototipo Competizione', this was an avant-garde creation in bright yellow, with wings on the nose and tail, a domed windscreen and gull-wing doors. It is believed to have been built on a Dino 206S racing chassis, renumbered 10523 by the factory before being sent to Pininfarina to be clothed in aluminium bodywork.

The Dino 206 GT was shown again at the Brussels Salon early in 1968 and went into production that year, with a total of 99 cars built by year end according to factory records. The model continued in production into 1969 – with a further 51 built – until superseded by the 246 GT, which was announced at the Turin Salon of that year.

At a glance there was little to signify the difference between the 2-litre 206 GT and the 2.4-litre 246 GT apart from the former's exposed fuel filler cap, but under the elegant skin there were significant changes. The 206 GT engine had an aluminium block, whereas the 246 GT used the Fiat-produced cast iron block. Wheelbase increased from 2280mm (89.8in) to 2340mm (92.1in) with a commensurate increase in length from 4150mm (163.4in) to 4230mm (166.5in). The new model, bodied in steel rather than aluminium, weighed 1080kg (2381lb) against 900kg (1984lb) for its predecessor, but its engine produced 195bhp at 7600rpm against the 206 GT's 180bhp at 7400rpm. The larger engine also provided a considerably better spread of torque, up from 138lb ft at 6500rpm to 166lb ft at 5500rpm, making the 246 GT much easier and more pleasant to drive.

These cars were never intended to be perceived as Ferraris, as the factory was trying to establish Dino as a marque in its own right. No 206 GT or 246 GT models ever carried any Ferrari badging from the factory. Any such identity, including *Cavallino Rampante* badges, found on these cars nowadays was fitted by dealers, concessionaires or subsequent owners. It was not until slow sales of the Dino 308 GT4 prompted Ferrari to rethink this philosophy that Dino badges were abandoned for Ferrari ones.

All Dino 206 GTs were left-hand drive, and, like early 246 GTs, featured 'knock-off' wheels with single triple-ear wheel retaining nuts, but in 1970 the 246 GT received wheels with five-bolt fixings, of a design identical to those used on Fiat Dinos except for having 'Dino' script instead of 'Fiat' cast into the rim. A right-hand drive version of the 246 GT became available in 1970, the earliest known chassis number being 01134.

A model for the US market was added in 1972, the earliest known chassis number being 02866. And also in 1972, at the Geneva Salon, the 246 GTS – with removable 'targa' roof – was introduced to complement the coupé, the earliest known chassis number of this variant being 03762. The open and closed models continued in production until 1974 with only minor changes to specification through the entire production period, relating mainly to lock barrel positions, brake scoop shape and size, headrest location, number plate light location and the type of metal used in the manufacture of the body panels.

Dinos had their own even-numbered chassis sequence, separate from the odd-numbered system used on Ferrari road cars of that period. This even-numbered sequence carried through into the Dino 308 GT4 models, which retained it until they ceased production in 1980. Although launched five years before this, in 1975, the 308 GTB and subsequent models were deemed part of mainstream production and followed the standard odd-numbered sequence up to chassis number 75000, after which odd and even numbers were used for all road models.

The Dino V6 element in this story is important because the V8 models evolved from it in a logical quest for more power, to keep performance on a par or ahead of their competitors. From 1974 to 1989 all roadgoing V8 models, apart from the limited-production 288 GTO and F40, maintained the unitary arrangement of transverse engine, transmission and final drive that had been introduced on the 206 GT in 1968.

During the period of transverse V8 production, Ferrari also developed a front-engined application for the Lancia Thema 8.32 luxury saloon, which featured a badge on its intake box reading 'Lancia by Ferrari'. This engine had type reference F105L, a capacity of 2927cc, fuel injection, dry-sump lubrication and a quoted power output of 215bhp. This engine was fitted with a 90° crankshaft as opposed to the 180° 'flat

HD-ZA196

Four variations on mid-engined V8 theme, part one: 308 GTB Group 4 rally car (top left), in livery used by Jean-Claude Andruet for Pozzi team in 1981; brutal twin-turbo Carma FF racer (top right) with 308 heritage discernible around cabin; four-wheel drive prototypes (above left) of 1988 with Alcan-developed aluminium chassis, wrongly predicted in magazines to be 328 replacement; normally aspirated 308 GT/M (above right) looks similar to scaled-down Le Mans Boxer.

plane' crankshaft of all other Ferrari V8 engines. The change resulted in an engine that was neither as smooth as the 'pure' unit nor able to rev as high. There were no Ferrari badges externally, only discreet yellow '8.32' motifs on the grille and, on first-series models, the sills just forward of the rear wheel arches. Second-series models, featuring a redesigned grille and front lights, displayed only the grille badge.

Ferrari also provided Lancia with a V8 engine for its World Sports Car Championship contender in 1983. With twin KKK turbochargers, the 2955cc engine in this Group C LC2 model produced around 620bhp. This Lancia confection had been preceded by the legendary Stratos – powered by the transverse Dino V6 engine – that swept all before it in international rallying through the 1973-78 period.

Although the factory never carried out any official competition development of its mainstream V8 road cars, plenty of privateers had a go. The firm of Michelotto in Padova (Padua) was routinely involved in small-scale development work for Ferrari, and a car with modifications by Michelotto could almost be regarded as 'works'. Michelotto's most notable V8 activity was to prepare 308 GTBs for rallying, and these achieved considerable success all over Europe during 1981-82. Cars entered by French importer Charles Pozzi, with Jean-Claude Andruet as his star driver, took victories in 1981 in the Targa Florio, Four Seasons, 24 Hours of Ypres and Tour de France, and in the Tour de France again in 1982.

Another Michelotto creation was the 308 GT/M, which appeared in 1984 and resembled a scaled-down Le Mans Boxer. Its naturally aspirated, longitudinally aligned V8 engine was mated to a Hewland transmission and mounted in a specially constructed tubular chassis, clothed with bodywork in composite materials. From this car's shape, mechanical configuration and use of composite materials, one can see its influences on the subsequent 288 Evoluzione prototypes and the F40. The chassis numbers of the three examples built – 001, 002 and 003 – did not follow Ferrari's standard sequence, so these should probably be considered Michelotto identities as the cars were constructed entirely at his own workshops, albeit with factory input and approval.

In 1974 Luigi Chinetti, the American importer, entered a heavily modified 308 GT4 at Le Mans, based on chassis number 08020, but an early retirement was all he had to show for the venture. It was entered again in 1975, but the organisers deemed that it had not been quick enough in practice to qualify. Chinetti tried unsuccessfully to dispute this verdict,

Four variations on mid-engined V8 theme, part two: wild 308-based creations by Willy Koenig (top left and top right), whose German tuning concern has customised many V8 and V12 Ferraris, mechanically and bodily, although their visual success must be a matter of personal taste; Zagato modified some 348s (above left and above right), with that coachbuilder's traditional 'double-bubble' roof plus Plexiglas engine cover and round tail lights, the latter pre-empting Ferrari's return to this style for the F355.

but the organisers would not relent and Chinetti withdrew his other entries in protest.

During 1977 Ferrari commissioned Pininfarina to build a lightweight development body for a 308 GTB (chassis number 22711), whose main identifying features were riveted wheel arch extensions and a pronounced front spoiler. It was painted in a red, white and green colour scheme, echoing that used on contemporary Formula 1 Ferraris. The car was under the wing of the factory's experimental department and bore the designation 308 GTB4 on its body sides and front spoiler. There has never been an official explanation of the project's purpose, although it would probably be reasonable to assume that the '4' in the title referred to the FIA Group 4 competition class. The project was soon abandoned, and the development engine replaced with a standard unit, before this unique car was sold to Garage Francorchamps in Belgium, which in turn sold it to a Belgian collector.

The only other V8-engined competition contemporaries were two hybrids produced by Carlo Facetti in Italy. The first was his brutal Carma FF 308 twin-turbo 1980 World Endurance Championship contender, based on a 308 GTB. This was extremely rapid, always posting good practice times, but unfortunately 'endurance' was not its strong point. In 1988 he campaigned an Alba with Ferrari V8 power in the IMSA GT Championship's Camel Light class in the US, but this was a pure sports racing car rather than a road car development. Also in similar vein were the Spice-Ferraris campaigned in the same series.

At the 1976 Turin Salon, Bertone produced a two-seater V8 Ferrari concept car that it named the Rainbow, due to its pivoting targa roof which retracted behind the seats when not in use, providing an almost instant transformation between open and closed motoring. The car was based on a 308 GT4 chassis reduced in wheelbase by 100mm (3.9in), and featured very angular shapes that even extended to the wheel arch profiles and wheel hub design.

In 1987 the Idea Studio of Turin designed a one-off Ferrari for the PPG paint group, sponsor of the Indycar World Series in the US. Based on a Mondial chassis, this was a fully functioning concept car and rolling laboratory to test new materials, and PPG used it as the official race pace car during 1988. Visually, this creation was an awkward blend of curves at the front and angles at the rear, with a lower ribbed section that extended from either side of the front grille opening, around the complete perimeter of the car.

At around the same time, Ferrari, in collaboration with the Alcan company of Canada, produced a pair

F355 Berlinetta clearly shows styling differences from preceding 348, notably in new wheel design, round tail light assemblies and loss of side intake strakes.

of mid-engined V8 prototypes with aluminium chassis and four-wheel drive. They were seen around the roads of Maranello during 1988, and pictures appeared in some magazines, but they were basically rolling test-beds and to date nothing has evolved from the concept. It certainly does not seem likely that four-wheel drive will ever by adopted by Ferrari, the vogue for that having already begun to fade when these cars were developed.

Numerous companies and individuals have tuned, turbocharged and bodily modified V8 models over the 20-year production span covered in this book. However, none has been factory approved and therefore they all lie outside the scope of an *Original* book. The more outrageous and bizarre efforts seem to have emanated from Germany, where Willy Koenig produced turbocharged models with wild body appendages, Lorenz & Rankel decapitated 308s to produce spider versions, Zender offered a range of body kits and Michalak produced the 348-based Conciso. Similarly, some cars have been heavily modified for club competition and track use, particularly in the UK for the Maranello Ferrari Challenge, organised by the Ferrari Owners Club.

The models covered in the following chapters were succeeded in 1994 by the most recent heir to the Ferrari V8 throne, the F355, which is available in Berlinetta (coupé), GTS (targa) and Spider forms. This model is a direct development from the 348, in overall mechanical configuration and general body shape, although most people find the revised lines much more pleasing.

In the mechanical department the engine was enlarged to 3.5 litres and fitted with five valves per cylinder – hence the 355 designation – while the gearbox now had six forward ratios. Maximum torque was 268lb ft (37kgm) at 6000rpm, but the really staggering figure was maximum power of 380bhp at a heady 8250rpm. This equates to a specific output of 109bhp per litre, better than any other normally aspirated contemporary, eclipsing even the 6.1-litre McLaren F1 (103bhp per litre).

The nose of the F355 features a grille that reflects the shape of the V12-powered 456 GT, F512M and 550 Maranello sister models, with small, circular, high-intensity daytime flasher lights either side of it. The 348's side strakes over the door radiator openings have been replaced by uncovered openings, the tail panel has a prominent upturned lip spoiler, and the 348's rectangular rear light clusters under a grille have been replaced by twin circular units on each side of a plain panel, reminiscent of the earlier 308/328

Front view of UK-registered F355, seen at Maranello Sales Ltd, shows grille treatment bearing closer resemblance to other models in Ferrari's range. F355 designation indicates a 3.5-litre engine and five valves per cylinder.

models. The road wheels are a five-spoke design, reflecting the same family heritage as the grille.

Without exception, the F355 has received huge praise in the world's motoring press, not only for its magnificent lines and impressive performance, but also for its driveability and usability. With much lighter and more user-friendly controls, it is a car that any driver can handle competently and confidently.

As I write this, rumours are rife of a front-engined replacement, which would break one of the main design threads shared by the V8-powered models in this book. But then rumours are all part of Ferrari's magic. Ferrari would not be Ferrari without them...

308 GT4 (1974-80)

High-level views of 308 GT4 emphasise Bertone's tight, clean lines, with elegant aluminium-framed glass areas flowing into boomerang-shaped air intakes in the rear pillars. Horizontal Dino badge on the nose indicates that this is a Series 1 car. In the USA, three series of models are referred to. Cosmetic changes to the bumpers and insignia on what were originally Series 1 cars initiated the USA Series 2 cars, prior to the arrival of the fully facelifted model, which became their Series 3 car.

The Dino 308 GT4 made its public debut at the Paris Salon in October 1973 as a new 2+2 to supplement the Dino 246 GT models that continued in production concurrently during 1974. Aesthetically the newcomer was very different from its stablemate, the flowing, voluptuous Pininfarina curves of the 246 replaced by a distinctive, sharp-edged wedge shape from the pen of Bertone.

No-one really seems to know Ferrari's exact reasons for abandoning Pininfarina – the time-honoured stylist for the products of Maranello – on this occasion. One school of thought relates it to the existence at the Ferrari factory of a production line for the Bertone-designed Fiat Dino, another speculates that Pininfarina did not have the capacity to produce a design due to its workload at the time, while yet another theory suggests that Bertone's involvement was instigated by the Fiat hierarchy. Whatever the real reason, it was a Bertone-designed model that graced the Ferrari stand in Paris that autumn. Prior to this commission, Bertone had only produced three bodies for Ferrari – a show car for the 1950 Geneva Salon and two one-off specials in the early 1960s based on 250 GT chassis.

Initial reaction to the styling of the 308 GT4 was not particularly favourable, as it was so different from the much-loved 246 GT and had a relatively conservative flavour. There were also echoes in the body details from other Bertone designs, the rear wing line being reminiscent of the Lancia Stratos and the overall profile akin to the Lamborghini Urraco. This similarity was not so surprising, as Bertone was trying to meet very similar and exacting specification requirements with all three cars, but it nevertheless influenced reaction to the new Dino.

Despite criticism of the new model's mundane appearance and lack of individuality, the 308 GT4 was a cleverly executed solution to the problem of how to combine 2+2 seating with a mid-engined configuration in a 2550mm (100.4in) wheelbase, which was only 210mm (8.3in) more than that of the compact two-seater Dino 246 GT.

The 308 GT4's transverse 3-litre engine was the first production Ferrari V8, although the company was no newcomer to this configuration on the competition front. The new engine/gearbox/differential arrangement was similar to that of the Dino 246 GT, being of unitary construction with the gearbox mounted under the engine. The 90° V8 had belt-driven twin overhead camshafts per bank, with four twin-choke Weber carburettors in the centre of the vee and exhausts on the outside. Compared with the Dino 246 GT, two extra cylinders and another half-litre in capacity saw a considerable increase in power

Optional Equipment

Series 1
Electric windows
Metallic paint
Heated rear window
Leather interior
Tinted glass
Wide wheels
Air conditioning
Sunroof
'Boxer' paint finish

Series 2
Metallic paint
Leather interior
Wide wheels
Air conditioning
Sunroof
'Boxer' paint finish

and torque, resulting in a rather more user-friendly overall package.

This was the first Ferrari to be made readily available to journalists, most previous full-scale road tests having been carried out with privately owned cars. Once press people had the opportunity to drive the 308 GT4, and to sample its superior performance and driveability compared with the Dino 246 GT, together with its excellent handling and practicality, their initial scepticism abated and praise for the car's virtues was more forthcoming.

The body styling still did not receive particular acclaim, although, with hindsight, Bertone provided an elegant solution to a difficult set of design parameters. This achievement was more appreciated when the car's Pininfarina-designed successor, the Mondial 8, was announced in 1980. When the 308 GT4's design is examined closely, some pleasing details are noticed, such as the boomerang-shaped intakes on the rear quarter panels, the flat, tunnelled rear screen, and the elegant simplicity of the instrument panel.

The 308 GT4 underwent various cosmetic changes during its six-year production period, but there were relatively few modifications under the engine cover. Essentially there are two generations of 308 GT4, commonly referred to as Series 1 (deep front grille) and Series 2 (full-width front grille). Perhaps the most significant post-launch development, however, was the introduction of a 2-litre 'tax break' 208 GT4 for the Italian market, but this version was not offered for sale in any other country.

Early 308 GT4s were badged solely as Dinos, carrying no Ferrari insignia on the bodywork or in the interior. In 1975, however, the cars were re-identified as Ferraris due to flagging sales, particularly in the US, where this model was the only Ferrari-made product available – and yet it did not even wear a Ferrari badge! Apart from the stylised chrome Dino 308 GT4 badge on the rear boot lid, the Dino identity disappeared hereafter. This change of strategy, however, did not lead to any alteration to the Dino chassis numbering system, the sequence continuing in its specific even-numbered series – created for the Dino 246 GT – right to the end of production, even when 308 GT4s were being built alongside 308 GTB/S models carrying chassis numbers in Ferrari's odd-number sequence.

Body & Chassis

The 308 GT4, like all Ferraris of the period (and some of the models still in current production), had a separate chassis rather than the unitary construction used by most manufacturers.

Further evidence that this is a Series 1 is provided by grille style and auxiliary driving lights outboard of it, while optional five-spoke wide wheels give a more aggressive stance from this angle. From rear, note flat, deeply tunnelled rear screen, rear wing line reminiscent of Lancia Stratos (another Bertone design) and light assemblies unique to 308 GT4, comprising three removable circular lenses in trapezoidal reflector surround.

Pair of Series 2 308 GT4s, showing revised full-width grille housing auxiliary lights. Blue car (Blu Sera) wears optional Campagnolo five-spoke wide wheels, yellow one (Giallo Fly) standard exposed-bolt Cromodora wheels; on Series 1 cars Cromodora wheels had small hub caps over bolts.

Dimensions & Weights

	Europe	US
Overall length	4300mm (169.3in)	4495mm (177.0in)
Overall width	1710mm (67.3in)	1710mm (67.3in)
Overall height	1210mm (47.6in)	1210mm (47.6in)
Wheelbase	2550mm (100.4in)	2550mm (100.4in)
Front track	1460mm (57.5in)	1460mm (57.5in)
Rear track	1460mm (57.5in)	1460mm (57.5in)
Dry weight (308)	1360kg (2998lb)	1450kg (3197lb)
Dry weight (208)	1305kg (2876lb)	–

The central chassis section under the cabin was constructed from large-section oval steel tubes, which also extended fore and aft to pick up front and rear suspension frames and engine mountings. Supplementary frames for suspension, steering, engine, door posts, body mounting and bumpers were constructed from rectangular-section and square-section steel tubes. US models had additional bracing for bumper mounting points and also between the engine and passenger compartment, to satisfy that country's more stringent crash test legislation.

The floor pan, inner wheel arches and front bulkhead were made of glass-fibre, bonded to the chassis. The engine/cabin firewall was steel with an aluminium foil blanket on the engine side. The rear boot floor was a steel sandwich construction with an insulating infill to reduce heat transfer from the exhaust silencer immediately below. A flat aluminium sheet undertray, with an access panel under the throttle pedal for cable replacement, extended from the front of the car almost to the end of the cabin section, and was attached by pop rivets. Front and rear towing eyes were attached to the chassis, on the right-hand side of the car under the valances.

The main body panels were steel pressings. Some, such as the large rear wing and roof quarter panel section, were made up of a number of smaller pressings welded together to form a single assembly. The only non-steel outer panels were the front bonnet cover and rear engine lid, which were aluminium panels over a steel frame, and the front grille surround panel, which was moulded in glass-fibre.

BODY TRIM & FITTINGS

The main items of bright trim – in polished aluminium – were the surrounds to the windscreen, door glasses and rear quarter windows, and the side gutter channel covers. The rectangular door handles, identical to those fitted on the Fiat X1/9 and Lamborghini Urraco, were chrome-plated zinc castings recessed in the door panel.

The glass was initially plain as standard, although tinted glass was available as an option until it became standard for Series 2 cars. Similarly, a heated rear screen was an option on Series 1s but standard on Series 2s. When tinted glass was fitted, the windscreen had heavy tinting along its upper edge. Windscreen wipers parked on the left on right-hand drive models, and on the right on left-hand drive cars. Unlike the other windows, the rear screen had a plain black rubber surround.

European Series 1s had no external mirrors, but US versions had a single, rectangular, chrome-plated mirror on the driver's door. European Series 2s had a single, oval, matt black plastic 'California' mirror manufactured by Vitaloni on the driver's door, with the option of a matching one on the passenger's door.

European models had full-width front and rear bumpers normally made of chromed steel, with a black rubber face over the entire width and depth. The front bumper incorporated rectangular side/turn lights, identical to those of the Lancia Beta saloon, while the rear one contained twin rectangular reversing lights. For a period during the production run the factory experienced supply difficulties and the chromed steel bumpers had to be temporarily substituted by matt black glass-fibre bumpers. It is impossible to pinpoint how many cars had glass-fibre bumpers, as these were also available as spare parts and steel-bumpered cars may have had them fitted, perhaps after an accident, during this phase.

This shot of a US version of the 308 GT4 shows main visual differences from European counterparts. Heavier bumper assemblies and side marker lights do nothing to enhance the lines.

Original horizontal Dino nose badge of Series 1 cars was replaced by familiar vertical Ferrari badge for Series 2s. Appropriate script badge was only identification factory ever fitted to rear of the car, apart from Cavallino Rampante on post-1975 US models.

Italian market 208 GT4 Series 1s wear the same Cromodora wheels (with small hubcaps) as equivalent 308 versions, but can be distinguished from the front by narrow grille and lack of auxiliary driving lights. From rear, note single tail-pipe and silencer shroud panel – but Ferrari badges are non-original additions.

The much more pronounced bumpers on US versions did nothing to enhance the lines of the car. Painted matt black, these heavy assemblies were made of steel and fitted with rubber faces and plastic end caps, which extended round the wing corners at front and rear. Amber side/turn light assemblies were recessed into the lower edge of the front bumper, while at the rear a single central reversing light was fixed to the lower edge of the bumper.

US models also had mandatory front and rear rectangular side marker lights cut into the wings, breaking the fluidity of line even more. On US Series 2s the full-width grille and shaped front panel harmonised better with the bumper, but the appearance was still ungainly. Legislation in the US also decreed that there was a louvred protection panel under the rear valance to shield the exhaust silencer. Japanese market cars also sported the undesirable appendages of US models.

All Series 1s originally carried Dino badging only, with no mention of Ferrari. The recessed enamel motif on the nose panel was a 'horizontal' rectangle for the Dino, in contrast to the 'vertical' form of Ferrari's usual *Cavallino Rampante* nose badge. Circular plastic Dino badges decorated the hub caps, and a chromed zinc script badge on the rear top edge of the boot lid read 'Dino 308 GT4'. The only other badge was a rectangular 'Disegno Bertone' motif mounted low between the door and rear wheel arch on the right-hand side.

In July 1975 Ferrari issued a directive to US dealers on the re-identification of existing stocks of Dino-badged cars. This gave instructions to fit an enamel Ferrari badge above the Dino badge on the nose of the car, to replace the Dino horn push with a button bearing the *Cavallino Rampante*, and to fix a chromed *Cavallino Rampante* to the tail panel.

All Series 2s bore some Ferrari identity from the factory. The enamel badge on the nose changed to the Ferrari style, either recessed or surface-mounted, but the tail badging stayed the same. On US versions a chromed *Cavallino Rampante* was added to the rear panel to the right of the number plate recess.

This image enhancement was intended to improve sales, which had been disappointing. To further this end, some concessionaires and dealers added more Ferrari badges. The normal post-factory additions were a chrome-plated Ferrari script under the rear number plate position and/or a *Cavallino Rampante* on the rear panel, as on the US version.

The front radiator grille on Series 1s was a horizontal, narrow-slat design in plain aluminium on European cars or matt black on US models. European cars had rectangular auxiliary lights mounted in recesses in the surround panel, but US versions and Italian 208 GT4 models lacked these. Series 2s had a full-width egg-crate grille in plain aluminium for all markets. As part of that identification change programme, late Series 1s for the US were given a small spoiler along the bottom of the front valance, and the bumpers were fitted with altered impact absorbers to slightly reduce their protrusion.

The front lid incorporated a slatted outlet for radiator air, and the engine lid carried a similar outlet. These were finished in matt black on 308 GT4s but plain aluminium on Italian market 208 GT4s. The front lid was released by a horizontal lever mounted on the driver's side wheel arch in the cabin, the engine and rear luggage compartment lids by twin, lockable, vertical, chromed levers in the driver's door shut post. Emergency pulls were also provided in case any of these three cables should break.

A factory-fitted manually operated steel sunroof was available as an option; in time this became a corrosion black spot, resulting in replacement of the whole roof panel. The fuel filler was recessed behind a hinged flap on the left-hand rear roof pillar, irrespective of market, and fed twin tanks mounted either side of the engine, with an interconnecting balance pipe between them.

PAINTWORK

During the 308 GT4 period the factory used acrylic paint produced by Glidden Salchi of Milan, and the full Ferrari colour range – 11 solid colours and 10 two-pack metallic finishes – was available for the Dino model.

US models had matt black front and rear valance panels, and from the late Series 1 period many cars were given what was described as the 'Boxer' paint finish, which was also available on European models to order. This consisted of a matt black lower half up to the waist crease, finished with a pinstripe. The 'Boxer' term referred to the 365/512 Berlinetta Boxer models, which had this paint finish as standard.

Most European models had a black underseal finish to the sills, forming a straight line on the lower edge of the doors between the front and rear wheel arches. However, some cars do not have this feature, and even in factory sales catalogues there is no consistency on this point.

INTERIOR TRIM & FITTINGS

The standard seats were trimmed in vinyl with cloth for the centre sections and head restraints, though early examples also had cloth covered side bolsters. The same cloth was used to face the roomy door pockets, with the remainder of the interior panelling matching the vinyl of the seats, except that the dashboard covering was always black vinyl for anti-glare reasons. A full leather interior was available as an option.

The bucket-style reclining front seats were fully adjustable, and had deep-sided squabs for good lateral location. Bucket-style seats were also used in the rear, but with limited headroom and even more limited legroom they were really only suitable for children on journeys of any duration. Customers could specify a trimmed luggage platform in place of these seats, although very few took up this option. All four seats were fitted with seat belts, the type depending upon market destination.

The floor, inner sills and wheel arches were fully carpeted in a colour compatible with the interior trim, chosen from a range of five colours. The carpet in the driver's footwell was protected by a black rubber heel mat. Series 1s had manual door windows with the option of electric operation, while Series 2s had standard electric door windows. In case of electric motor failure, a small crank handle was provided to effect manual operation, by removing a small plug from the door panel and inserting the handle. A small circular red warning light was fitted in the trailing edge of each door, and the door pockets incorporated interior lights.

The open-gate gearchange was positioned on the driver's side of the central tunnel, with the gate flush to the tunnel top for left-hand drive or recessed in a cut-out in the tunnel top and side for right-hand drive. Provision was made for a vertical radio installation at the front corner of the tunnel, with speakers in the front of the door panels. Rectangular ashtrays were provided on the tunnel for both front and rear passengers, with a cigarette lighter to the rear of the front ashtray. The tunnel also housed the handbrake between the front seats.

The Momo steering wheel had three aluminium spokes, a leather rim and a central horn push bearing a Dino badge (Series 1) or a *Cavallino Rampante* (Series 2). The roof lining was white vinyl, ribbed in the flat centre section and with padded bolster sections around the perimeter, those at the front incorporating recesses for the sun visors, the passenger's including a vanity mirror. An interior light was fitted at the back of the roof lining. The dipping interior mirror was fixed to the windscreen with an adhesive pad.

One other option was air conditioning, which fed through the standard heating and ventilation system. The pump was mounted in the engine compartment and belt-driven from the engine.

Front cabin area gives plenty of space for driver and passenger, but rear legroom is severely limited for adults on all but short journeys. On this right-hand drive 308 GT4 outer panels of front seats have been re-trimmed with cloth; originally they would have been vinyl, as on rear seats. Comparison of centre consoles for left-hand drive (upper) and right-hand drive (lower) shows recessed gearchange gate unique to right-hand drive cars. Correct vinyl seat bolster trim is seen on left-hand drive car.

BODY COLOURS

Solid colours	Code
Rosso Chiaro	20.3.90
Rosso Dino	20.3.350
Blu Scurro Dino	20.A.357
Azzurro Dino	20.A.349
Verde Germoglio	20.G.465
Giallo Senappe	20.Y.464
Nuovo Giallo Fly	20.Y.490
Giallo Dino	20.Y.348
Bianco Polo Park	20.W.152
Nero	N/A
Bleu Montecarlo	N/A

Metallic colours	Code
Verde Pino	N/A
Verde Medio	N/A
Blu Dino	N/A
Blu Sera	N/A
Azzurro Metalizzato	N/A
Marrone Dino	N/A
Grigio Ferro	N/A
Oro Chiaro	N/A
Argento Auteil	N/A
Rosso Rubino	N/A

Note
Optional 'Boxer' colour scheme had matt black lower body (code 20.B.50 plus 20.T.380 matt lacquer).

Clean dashboard layout, with 'butterfly' wings at extremities to throw switchgear closer to driver's hands. This design was more practical and easier to read than that on succeeding 308 GTB. Speedometer and rev counter swapped positions for right-hand drive. Cavallino Rampante horn push was a feature of Series 2 models; Series 1s had Dino motif instead.

Dashboard & Instruments

The instrument panel was a very simple design, slim and rectangular in shape with angled wings at the extremities to bring the switchgear closer to the driver. The panel was finished in matt aluminium on 308 GT4s and matt black on 208 GT4s.

The Veglia-Borletti dials, all with white markings on black faces, were mounted in the centre section of the panel, immediately in front of the driver. They comprised two large dials for speedometer and rev counter, with three small dials in a triangle between them for oil pressure (top left), water temperature (top right) and clock (bottom centre), and two small dials outside them for fuel (left) and oil temperature (right). The 280kph or 180mph speedometer incorporated the distance recorder and a trip meter, while the 10,000rpm rev counter had warning sectors in orange from 7000rpm and red from 7700rpm. The speedometer and rev counter swapped places for left-hand and right-hand drive, so that the speedometer was always in the outboard position.

The inboard wing of the panel contained three sliding levers for the heating and ventilation system. The outer levers controlled distribution to the left-hand and right-hand sides of the car, while the centre lever set the heat. The outboard wing contained a row of three switches across the top with respective warning lights below them, the functions being (from the inboard end) auxiliary lights, hazard warning lights and defroster fan. US versions also had a 'fasten seat belts' warning light that worked in conjunction with a buzzer when the ignition was on and the belt buckle uncoupled.

The lights were controlled by a stalk on the left of the steering column, with a second smaller stalk on the same side for the direction indicators. A right-hand column stalk operated the windscreen wipers (two-speed plus intermittent) and washers.

Three circular demister outlets were positioned centrally in the top of the dashboard. When air conditioning was fitted on Series 1 cars, it discharged through these vents, which in practice turned out to provide poor circulation. A factory technical bulletin was issued in 1975, effecting a modification to solve the problem by discharging air through the footwell outlets, and all subsequent air-conditioned cars had this configuration.

Air conditioning, when fitted, was controlled by two dial switches on the central tunnel, for temperature and fan speed. Switches for the electric windows, again when fitted, were alongside the gearchange gate on the tunnel, while the choke slide control was alongside the handbrake.

On the passenger side of the dashboard was a useful lockable glovebox. Below this was the fuse board, behind a screwed panel trimmed in black vinyl to match the dashboard covering.

Luggage Compartment

The main luggage storage area was in a separate compartment to the rear of the engine. This was fully lined, including on the underside of the lid, with a heavy-duty carpet in a check design that combined black with red, beige, tan or blue, depending upon interior carpet colour. The boot was a usefully rectangular shape, but rather shallow, and care had to be taken not to use it for items that might be affected by heat from the exhaust silencer immediately underneath and the engine ahead.

Upholstery Colours

Cloth/vinyl [1]	Code
Red	–
Beige	–
Tan	–
Black	–
Navy Blue [2]	–

[1] Contrast colour combinations of cloth and vinyl could be specially ordered; eg, Navy Blue cloth with Beige vinyl.
[2] With Navy Blue cloth, Light Blue vinyl was a standard alternative to Navy Blue vinyl.

Leather	Code
Grigio	VM3393
Nero	VM8500
Beige	VM4208
Crema	VM3997
Rosso	VM3171
Blu	VM3282

Carpets	Code
Nero	80
Rosso	81
Testa di Moro	83
Blu	84
Bruciato	85

Rear boot compartment – seen with correct carpet weave – is convenient rectangular shape of reasonable size, but care must be taken not to load items that may be affected by heat, due to exhaust silencer immediately below and engine ahead. Front compartment, with spacesaver spare wheel, leaves little room for anything other than small, soft bags; with full-size spare wheel, mandatory in the US, even this space disappeared.

Tool Kit

Bag 1
- Carburettor spanner
- Range of eight open-end spanners, 6-22mm
- Pliers, 180mm long
- Flat-blade screwdriver, 120mm long
- Flat-blade screwdriver, 150mm long
- Philips screwdriver, 4mm diameter
- Philips screwdriver, 5-9mm diameter
- Spark plug spanner
- Short extension for exhaust gas analyser for rear manifold of cylinders 1, 2, 3 (US/Australia only).
- Short extension for exhaust gas analyser for rear manifold of cylinder 4 (US/Australia only).

Bag 2
- Scissor-type jack with ratchet drive
- Wheel nut spanner
- Alternator belt
- Air conditioning compressor belt (where fitted)
- Air pump control belts (US/Australia only)
- Emergency hazard warning triangle (Europe)
- Set of fuses
- Set of bulbs
- Spark plugs (2)

The front compartment had little space for luggage as it housed the spare wheel, a spacesaver for all markets except the US, which required a standard road wheel.Viewed from the front of the car, the front corners of the compartment contained the battery on the left and the air horn pump and screen washer bottle on the right, the horns themselves being between the radiator and grille. A plastic shield covered the brake master cylinder and servo so that any remaining space stayed clean, and could be used for stowing soft items.

A comprehensive tool kit was supplied in two soft vinyl bags, mounted in the spare wheel well on European cars or in the right-hand corner of the boot for the US and Australian markets.The tools and spare parts provided are listed in the panel.

Engine

The 308 GT4's engine, Ferrari's first production V8, displaced 2926cc (178.6cu in) and had type reference F106AL.The 208 GT4 engine for the Italian market displaced 1991cc (121.5cu in) and had a different suffix to give type reference F106C.

The new engine shared similarities with its 12-cylinder relatives, the 308 version having the same 81mm (3.19in) by 71mm (2.79in) bore and stroke as the 365 series engines, as used in the Daytona among others, and the same basic architecture but with a 90° angle between the cylinder banks, light alloy construction with shrunk-in cast iron cylinder liners, and paired connecting rods on the crankshaft. For the GT4, however, the engine was mounted transversely ahead of the rear axle line, in unit with the gearbox and final drive assembly.The light alloy castings for the block, cylinder heads and sump were manufactured to a very high standard in Ferrari's own foundry and left in their natural dull finish.

Power output figures given by the factory varied through the life of the model, according to market destination and changing emissions legislation, which gradually became more widespread following its introduction in California in 1968.The pump for the air conditioning system, where fitted, also had a debilitating effect on the engine.

European Series 1s were quoted as producing maximum power of 250bhp (SAE) at 7700rpm and maximum torque of 210lb ft (29kgm) at 5000rpm. On US Series 1s the figures dropped to 240bhp (SAE) at 6600rpm and 195lb ft (27kgm) at 5000rpm. The figures for European Series 2s were initially unchanged from the Series 1s, but in 1978 maximum power fell to 230bhp at 7700rpm and maximum torque to 203lb ft (28.1kgm) at 4600rpm.At the same time US Series 2s had to be equipped with a catalytic converter and their figures dropped to 205bhp at 6600rpm and 181lb ft (25kgm) at 5000rpm. In all these cases the compression ratio remained at 8.8:1.

For the 208 GT4, which had a compression ratio of 9:1, the factory quoted maximum power of 180bhp at 7700rpm and maximum torque of 137lb ft (19kgm) at 4900rpm. On this engine the bore was reduced to 66.8mm (2.63in).

Each of the two cylinder heads had twin overhead camshafts machined from forged steel, the inner one actuating the inlet valves and the outer one the exhaust valves. The camshafts were supported on three journal bearings, the lower halves being part of the head casting while the upper halves were attached to the head by steel studs with nuts and washers. Camshaft drive on each head was via a toothed belt with tensioner within a cast aluminium belt cover, from a geared drive off the crankshaft on the right-hand end of the engine.

Distributor drive was taken off the left-hand end of both inlet camshafts on twin-distributor models, but only the forward inlet camshaft on single-distributor models. European Series 1 cars and all US and Australian cars had two Magneti Marelli S159A distributors (one for each bank of cylinders), while European Series 2 cars had a single Magneti Marelli S127G distributor until January 1978. After this date European cars were fitted with a Magneti Marelli AEI 200A inductive discharge electronic ignition system, utilising distributor type SM805A. The recommended sparking plugs were Champion N7Y for normal use or N6Y for continuous high-speed running, irrespective of model. The numbers for the cylinder firing order were cast into the aluminium camshaft covers close to the plug ports.

Engine bay is dominated by large crackle black air filter housing above carburettors; access to forward bank of cylinders is virtually impossible without its removal. Flexible hose at bottom left channels air to oil cooler, while oil filter is easily accessible in top of vee.

On each head the single inlet and exhaust valves were inclined at 46° degrees with respect to each other, and driven from their camshafts via bucket tappets with shim adjustment. Valve timing varied according to model and is given in a panel.

The light alloy pistons were flat-topped with a perimeter upstand incorporating cut-outs for valve clearance. Four piston rings were fitted, the bottom one for oil control. Forged steel connecting rods were paired, one from each bank, on a single crankshaft journal, with specially shaped big-end bolts to fit into cut-outs in the rod.

The crankshaft, also machined from forged steel, ran in five main bearings and had an eight-bolt flange at the left-hand end for connection to the steel flywheel. The camshaft drive gear keyed onto the shaft at the right-hand end, together with the main belt pulley. Small-end bearings were phosphor bronze, while big-end and main bearings were plain white metal. Bearing lubrication was via holes drilled in the crowns of the journals. The cast iron cylinder liners were a push-fit and had locating flanges that seated flush with the top of the block.

Engine lubrication was wet-sump by means of a gear-driven oil pump, with an easily accessible full-flow filter in the engine vee. An oil cooler was fitted on the left-hand side of the engine compartment, air being fed to it from the left-hand rear quarter intake. A crankcase emission control system was standard throughout the range, feeding oil vapour from the head breathers back into the air filter. With a warm engine, the oil pressure gauge should read between 6.5 bar (92.5psi) and 4.5 bar (64.0psi).

All models used four Weber twin-choke 40 DCNF carburettors, but to varying specifications as follows: 35/36/37/38 for European twin-distributor models, 57/58/59/60 for European single-distributor models, 45/46/47/48 for US versions and 64/65/66/67 for Australian variants. The carburettors were fed by a Corona electric fuel pump situated close to the fuel outlet of the left-hand tank, with filter adjacent.

Spanning the carburettors in the centre of the vee was a large air filter with a crackle black finished casing. It was connected to a large flexible hose feeding air from the right-hand boomerang-shaped intake in the rear quarter panel. The air filter was a washable (with petrol) cartridge, although the instruction in handbooks for US and Australian versions was to replace it every 15,000 miles, or sooner if the car was used in very dusty conditions.

The engine was water-cooled by a front radiator with twin thermostatically controlled electric fans. The fans were activated by a sensor in the base of the radiator if water temperature exceeded 84°C (183°F). Circulation was by a belt-driven water pump at the timing gear end of the engine, and this also fed water on demand to left-hand and right-hand heater radiators (one for each side of the car), which had individual fans mounted in the corners of the front

SYSTEM CAPACITIES (LITRES)

	Europe	US
Rear boot	250	190
Front boot	35	–
Fuel tanks	80	80
Cooling system	18	18
Washer bottle	1	1
Engine oil	9	9
Gearbox oil	4	4

Timing Data

	Twin distributor	Single distributor
308 GT4		
Inlet opens BTDC	34°	30°
Inlet closes ABDC	46°	50°
Exhaust opens BBDC	36°	36°
Exhaust closes ATDC	38°	28°
208 GT4		
Inlet opens BTDC	–	34°
Inlet closes ABDC	–	46°
Exhaust opens BBDC	–	40°
Exhaust closes ATDC	–	24°

Valve timing should be measured with a clearance of 0.50mm (0.020in) between the tappet thimbles and camshaft. Valve clearances with cold engine should be 0.20-0.25mm (0.008-0.010in) for inlet valves and 0.30-0.35mm (0.012-0.014in) for exhaust valves, measured between the valve pads and camshaft. Firing order is 1-5-3-7-4-8-2-6.

valance. A remote header tank was mounted in the right-hand corner of the engine compartment. The system was pressurised by 0.9 bar (12psi), and the recommended anti-freeze content was one-third for normal conditions. The thermostat, set to open at 80°C (176°F), was mounted in the water pump outlet housing on the right-hand side of the engine.

A single belt drove the water pump and alternator off the main crankshaft pulley, which was tensioned by adjusting the alternator position; the deflection, measured between the water pump and alternator pulleys, should not exceed 4.6mm (0.18in). A second groove on the crankshaft pulley drove the air conditioning compressor (where fitted), which had a slotted adjuster below it; the maximum deflection for this belt is 3mm (0.12in).

On European cars each bank of cylinders had a four-branch tubular steel exhaust manifold, whereas US and Australian models had pressed steel collector manifolds with air injection points. The forward manifold fed via a single pipe to a flanged connection into the right-hand side of the silencer box, while the rearward manifold fed in the same manner into the left-hand side of the silencer box. Heat shields were provided above both manifolds, and also below the forward one to protect the starter motor.

The silencer was transversely mounted across the tail of the car, under the boot floor. The exhaust gases exited through two pairs of chromed tail-pipes pointing directly rearward except on US models, which used tail-pipes with 90° bends to direct exhaust gases towards the ground. As this was not very pleasing aesthetically, Ferrari effected a modification in July 1975 – at the same time as the Ferrari badging directive – so that dummy tail-pipes shrouded the downward-facing pipes.

US and Australian models were fitted with an evaporative loss system and an emission control device that injected air into the exhaust valve ports.

Twin headlight pod: outer light is for dipped beam, inner one for main beam.

Transmission

The all-synchromesh five-speed gearbox was mounted in unit with the engine, clutch and differential assemblies, located below the engine to the rear of the sump. However, it did not share the engine oil for lubrication, having its own ribbed aluminium sump matching that of the engine.

The clutch, mounted on the flywheel on the left-hand end of the engine, was a mechanically operated, dry, single-plate diaphragm type of 9.5in (241mm) diameter, with an assister spring to reduce pedal pressure. Power was transmitted from the clutch shaft, through a triple transfer gear assembly on roller bearings, down to the gearbox main shaft. These components were housed at the left-hand end of the engine in an alloy casing with a removable cover.

The main shaft had first, reverse, second and third gears machined into it, with fourth and fifth gears keyed onto it. The gears were helical with Porsche-designed synchromesh, and the complete assembly ran in roller bearings. From the main shaft drive was transferred via the selected gear using forked selectors to the secondary shaft, from the centre of which was taken the gear drive to the limited slip differential. Solid drive shafts with constant velocity joints at each end were bolted to the differential couplings, and transmitted the drive to the rear wheels.

The gear selection linkage ran from the selector

Overall Gear Ratios

Gear	208 GT4	308 GT4
First	1:15.722	1:12.669 [1]
Second	1:10.823	1:8.719
Third	1:7.787	1:6.274
Fourth	1:5.722	1:4.611
Fifth	1:4.052	1:3.529
Reverse	1:14.936	1:12.036
Final Drive	15/69	17/63

[1] 1:13.297 for US/Australian versions

input shaft on the gearbox, under the engine, and to the gear lever. The gearchange pattern had a 'dog-leg' first (to the left and back) with reverse opposite, then two more planes for second/third and fourth/fifth. The speedometer drive was taken off the right-hand end of the gearbox, by cable up to chassis number 08198 and thereafter by electrical pulse transmission.

ELECTRICAL EQUIPMENT & LIGHTS

The electrical system was 12-volt, served from a 60Ah or 66Ah battery fed by a Bosch alternator. Specifications for all the major components are given in the panel.

Lighting equipment varied enormously according to market, although it was all of Carello manufacture. Twin headlights, with the outer units for dipped beam, were mounted in retractable pods contained in cut-outs in the front lid. The pods were raised by electric motors actuated by relays when the headlights were switched on, but there was manual back-up by means of a knurled knob on each motor. The bulbs were 55 watt quartz iodine filaments, as were those for the auxiliary lights (where fitted) either side of the radiator. Cars for the French market had yellow headlight lenses in line with that country's legislation at that time.

The front side/turn indicator lights on European cars had either clear or clear/amber lenses, again according to market. All US cars had amber front side/turn indicator lights, along with rectangular side marker lights in amber (front) or red (rear) set into the wings. European cars had small, circular, surface-mounted amber indicator repeaters on the front wings, just forward of the wheel arches. Japanese market cars had large rectangular indicator repeaters in the same location.

At the rear, trapezoidal assemblies housed three circular, separately removable lenses which covered, from the outboard end, the direction indicator (normally amber, but red on US cars), stop/tail light and reflector. On European cars two rectangular reversing lights were mounted in the rear bumper, while US cars had a single rectangular unit suspended centrally below the bumper. Number plate illumination was from a twin-bulb unit housed in the trailing lower edge of the boot lid.

The only notable change to the lighting during production was the relocation of the front auxiliary lights behind the full-width grille on Series 2 models. Auxiliary lights were never fitted to the US 308 GT4 or the Italian 208 GT4.

MAJOR ELECTRICAL EQUIPMENT

Battery	12V 60/66Ah
Alternator	Bosch 0.120.489.542
Voltage regulator (in alternator)	Bosch 0.19.20.52.004
Distributor (twin, Europe)	Marelli S159A
Distributor (single, Europe to 1/78)	Marelli S127G
Distributor (single, Europe from 1/78)	Marelli SM 805A
Distributor (208 GT4)	Marelli S159C
Distributor (US/Australia)	Marelli S159B
Coil (Ferrari modified)	Marelli BZR 201A
Coil (Europe from 1/78)	Marelli AEI 200A
Radiator fan motors	Lucas 9GM/54071553E
Windscreen wiper motor	Marelli TGE 140 BAK
Starter motor	F 4162784
Spark plugs (normal use)	Champion N7Y
Spark plugs (high speed)	Champion N6Y

Suspension views at front (top) and rear (above) show ventilated disc brakes and differing coil spring/shock absorber positions – within wishbones at front, above them at rear – that were to remain basically unchanged in concept for succeeding series of V8-powered models.

SUSPENSION & STEERING

Suspension was independent all round, each wheel having twin unequal-length wishbones in fabricated steel, a coil spring and a double-acting shock absorber. Anti-roll bars were fitted front and rear

The Koni shock absorbers, types 82x-1830 (front) and 82x-1831 (rear), were co-axially mounted within the coil springs. The spring/shock absorber units were

Suspension Settings

Front toe-in	1.0-3.0mm
Front camber	+0°10′ to +0°30′
Rear toe-in	2.0-4.0mm
Rear camber	−1°20′ to −1°40′

Fixed castor angle should be 4°. All settings are applicable to a car in static laden condition: full tank of petrol, two persons on board, 20kg of luggage.

mounted at an angle between the wishbones at the front, but vertically above the upper wishbone at the rear. All suspension units were mounted to the chassis through Teflon-lined bushes.

The front hub carriers were machined steel castings mounted between the wishbones on rubber bushed couplings, and they each incorporated a stub axle. Bolted to the stub axle was a steel hub assembly incorporating inner and outer roller-type wheel bearings. The brake disc was bolted to the hub, sandwiching the disc dust shroud.

The rear hub carriers were machined aluminium castings, each with a central hole through which the stub axle shaft passed to connect to the drive shaft, which had a retaining bolt at its inner end to hold it in place, together with the wheel bearings housed in the carrier. The brake disc was bolted to a circular flange on the outer end of the stub axle.

Steering was by rack and pinion, with 3.28 turns lock to lock and a turning circle of 12m (39ft). The steering ball joints were sealed units requiring no lubrication, with automatic slack take-up facility.

Brakes

ATE ventilated discs were fitted all round, of 10.75in (273mm) diameter and fitted with Ferodo 1/D332 pads. The system was servo-assisted, with a tandem master cylinder feeding independent circuits to the front and rear wheels. Each circuit had its own reservoir, mounted in the front luggage compartment under an access cover in the shield panel just forward of the windscreen.

The system was also equipped with a pressure-limiting valve to the rear circuit, and a dashboard warning light to advise of pressure loss in either circuit; this also served as the handbrake warning light. The handbrake was cable-operated to the calipers on the rear wheels, with a manual slack take-up adjuster on the assembly at the rear of the car.

Wheels & Tyres

The standard cast alloy wheels were very similar in design to those of the Dino 246 GT. On Series 1s the five fixing bolts were concealed behind a chromed hub cover with a plastic Dino badge in the centre, but on Series 2s the bolts were exposed and chromed, as on the 246 GT, and the central badge carried a *Cavallino Rampante*.

The wheels were manufactured by Cromodora, and finished in silver paint and lacquer. The manufacturer's name, Dino script and wheel size were cast in raised characters around the rim. Wider Campagnolo five-spoke alloy wheels could be specified as an option, and many customers chose these. Wheel and tyre specifications are given in the panel.

The spare wheel on European cars was a spacesaver type, but legislation required that US models had to have a full-size spare wheel.

Wheels/Tyres

Standard wheels	Cromodora 6.5J×14
Optional wheels	Campagnolo 7J×14
Tyres	Michelin XWX 205/70 VR14[1]
Spacesaver wheel (Europe only)	3.25×14
Spacesaver tyre (Europe only)	Michelin 105 R18

[1]These were the usual tyres, but Goodyear Grand Prix 800 205/70 VR14 were also supplied.

Identification Plates

Engine compartment
A plate was fixed to the engine block in the centre of the vee, at the cam belt drive end, giving the engine type number and individual serial number. An aluminium plate was fixed to the engine/boot bulkhead, giving the model homologation number, engine type number, chassis type number and individual chassis number. On the right-hand upper chassis tube, viewed from the rear of the car, the chassis type number and individual chassis number were stamped into the metal of the tube.

Interior (308 GT4 Europe)
On the driver's side door post was an aluminium plate identifying conformity with European standards. On the upper face of the steering column was an aluminium plate giving model type and individual chassis number. A windscreen sticker indicated recommended tyre pressures.

Interior (308 GT4 US)
On the driver's side door post was an FMV safety standard conformity plate, showing year and month of manufacture, gross vehicle weight, gross axle weight rating, individual chassis number, and car type. On the upper face of the steering column was an aluminium plate giving model type and individual chassis number. On the inside of the glovebox lid was a further FMV safety standard label, giving tyre data and car capacity.

Australian market cars had plates located as on the US version, but with details specific to that market, the door post plate being fitted to the cars upon arrival in Australia.

Aluminium 308 GT4 chassis plate in engine compartment, and original 208 GT4 windscreen sticker denoting tyre pressures – complete with dodgy English spellings!

Production Data

Model	Production period	Chassis number range	Number built
308 GT4	1974-80	07202-15604	2826
208 GT4	1975-80[1]	08830-15596	840

[1]One car produced in 1974.

308/328 SERIES (1975-89)

European glass-fibre 308 GTB with optional 'Boxer' paint finish and deep front spoiler, here in profile exemplifying Pininfarina's smooth lines and family relationship to 365/512 Berlinetta Boxer series.

The 308 GTB was presented to the world in October 1975 at the Paris Salon as the successor to the Dino 246 GT, to be produced concurrently with the Dino 308 GT4. The new model was badged entirely as a Ferrari from the outset, with no Dino reference whatsoever, and the chassis numbers were part of Ferrari's standard odd-number production car sequence.

Ferrari had returned to Pininfarina for the styling of the 308 GTB, and it pleased fans of the 246 Dino to see some of that model's visual elements appear on the new car. These included the tapering, scalloped air intakes carried along the door panels, the recessed, wrap-round rear screen, and the twin circular tail lamps. The nose received the then fashionable wedge treatment, but overall there was a pleasing balance between this feature and the car's flowing curves, creating a homogeneous design that would remain virtually unchanged for ten years. There was still a luggage compartment in the tail, although this time a single lid, hinged at the top of the roof pillars, covered both the luggage compartment and the engine bay; luggage was protected by a vinyl cover zipped around its perimeter.

What was not obvious to the observer was that the body was constructed from glass-fibre. The 308 GTB was the first production Ferrari to have a glass-fibre body, the alleged reason for the choice being that it was quicker and easier to have moulds made for glass-fibre than to make dies for metal pressings – slow 308 GT4 sales meant that Ferrari wanted to put the new model on the market as speedily as possible. The quality of the glass-fibre mouldings was very high, and many bodies are still in fine condition over 20 years later. These early glass-fibre models can be identified by an indented line where the roof joins the windscreen pillar.

In late 1976, without prior notification, US models started to be delivered with steel bodies, although glass-fibre cars continued to be supplied in Europe until the middle of 1977. Various reasons for the change have been speculated: that glass-fibre was only used as a temporary measure, to effect an earlier than planned model introduction; that the glass-fibre models were more labour-intensive and costly to produce than had been anticipated; and that Ferrari had difficulty finding specialists of adequate standard to repair accident damage.

In September 1977 a Spider version, the 308 GTS, was presented, with a black, vinyl-covered, removable roof section. The only other visible differences were vertically-slatted, lockable, hinged covers over the rear quarter windows, and the use of a GTS badge on the tail panel. The roof section, which could be stowed

Rear view of glass-fibre 308 GTB in 'Boxer' paint finish (above) clearly shows standard single exhaust tail-pipe arrangement found on European carburettor models (US versions had two pairs of twinned tail-pipes) and bumper-inset reversing lights (on US versions they were in the centre of the indicator lenses). Another European 308 GTB with Giallo Fly paintwork (right) has optional wide wheels and replacement four-outlet exhaust system; note single cut-out in rear valance, clearly visible in this body colour.

behind the seats when not in use, was easily removed by releasing two over-centre catches.

European models had a single left-hand exhaust tail-pipe from the transverse silencer box, whereas US versions had a pair of twinned tail-pipes protruding through either end of a slatted, matt black shield over the silencer assembly. A significant mechanical difference between the two markets was that US models continued with the wet-sump lubrication system of the 308 GT4, but European models had dry-sump lubrication. These differences continued until the arrival of the fuel-injected models – the 308 GTBi

Two views of cars in US guise. The side marker lights show up well on the black 308 GTSi, but some of the US-only tail features stand out better on the red steel-bodied 308 GTS: heavier bumpers, full-width row of louvres on the engine lid, reversing lights within the indicator lenses on carburettor models, and louvred shield for four-pipe exhaust.

QV (above, in GTS form) can be quickly identified by driving lights in grille extremities, rectangular indicator repeaters on front wings, radiator air outlet in front lid and paired door mirrors with small enamel Ferrari badges. From rear (right, in GTB form), note change of indicator lenses in comparison with early European carburettor models and plain rear bumper, bringing world-market models a little closer; high-intensity fog warning lights below bumper were not fitted to US variants, and this QV has optional rear spoiler.

and the 308 GTSi – in late 1980, when cars for all markets received the paired twin exhaust tail-pipes and wet-sump lubrication.

Fuel injection was introduced to meet increasingly stringent exhaust emissions legislation in the US, but the penalty, reduced power output, received wide coverage in the motoring press of the period. At the same time as the mechanical changes, modifications were made to the interior layout and the wheels were altered to a metric size – and slightly changed in design – to accommodate Michelin TRX tyres.

With the demise of the 208 GT4 in 1980, Ferrari dropped the 2-litre engine into the GTB/S bodyshells to produce the 208 GTB and 208 GTS 'tax-break' models for the Italian market only; these cars retained carburettors. At the Turin Salon in April 1982 a turbocharged version of the 208 GTB was announced, using a single exhaust-driven KKK turbocharger, Bosch K-Jetronic fuel injection and Marelli Digiplex electronic ignition. Apart from a 'turbo' badge on the tail panel, other visual differences were a NACA scoop on the lower body side in front of the rear wheel arch, a rear roof spoiler on the buttresses, and the paired twin exhaust pipes enclosed in a pair of chromed shrouds. Initially Ferrari proposed to produce the Turbo only as a GTB, but by 1983 a GTS version was also available.

That question of reduced power output on world-market 308 GTBi and GTSi models was also being addressed, and the public saw the fruits of this at the Paris Salon in October 1982, when the Quattrovalvole (QV) models were announced. The new four-valves-per-cylinder heads regained all the horsepower lost through emission control legislation, and more than satisfied the critics.

The QV models featured subtle styling changes to the exterior: a new front bumper and grille, an outlet grille in the front lid, new door mirrors and polished ridges on the wheels, plus the option of the roof spoiler as on the 208 Turbo. Internally there were minor changes, and cloth seat centres were available in place of full leather if required.

The final evolution of the series came with the 328 GTB and GTS models, announced at the 1985 Frankfurt Salon. They are instantly recognisable by their re-designed front and rear bumpers, front grille, and lower front and rear body panels; the latter give the car a more rounded appearance, softening the wedge profile. The new model also featured re-designed wheels, while the interior was changed comprehensively. Engine capacity increased to 3.2 litres, with power rising by 12 per cent and torque by 17 per cent.

The 328 models also spawned 2-litre turbocharged versions – again for the Italian market only – known simply as the GTB Turbo and GTS Turbo, which were announced at the 1986 Turin Salon. The new Turbo models was fitted with a Japanese IHI turbocharger and incorporated a Behr intercooler, which permitted a rise in boost pressure from 0.6 bar to 1.05 bar. Visually these models differed from the others, with a NACA duct in front of the rear wheel arch on the lower body side, a raised engine lid centre section with additional louvres, and a slotted rear bumper to aid engine bay heat dissipation.

The 328 GTB/S and GTB/S Turbo models were produced until 1989, when the replacement 348 series was announced.

Japanese market 308 GTB QV: front bumper and light lenses are similar to US model, although bumper protrusion is slightly less as it does not house impact-absorbing dampers required for US market. Indicator repeaters on front wings, however, mirror European QV style.

Body & Chassis

The separate chassis was constructed from large-section oval steel tubes, with rectangular and square ancillary tube fabrications to provide support for suspension, steering, bodywork and bumpers. For US models, additional bracing was provided, as it had been on the 308 GT4, to satisfy that market's more demanding crash test legislation.

The floor pan, inner wheel arches and front bulkhead were constructed from glass-fibre, bonded to the chassis members. The firewall between engine bay and cabin was constructed from sheet steel, with an aluminium foil blanket on the engine side. The floor of the rear luggage compartment comprised two layers of steel sheet with insulation between them. A flat sheet metal undertray extended from the front axle line to the rear of the cabin, tack-welded to the chassis tubes.

Chassis construction retained the same configuration and components throughout the life of the 308 and 328 series. It was basically identical to that of the 308 GT4, except for a reduced wheelbase of 2340mm (92.1in) – the same as that of the Dino 246 GT.

The first 308 GTB models had bodies constructed almost entirely from glass-fibre, the only metal panel being the front luggage compartment lid, which was in aluminium on a steel frame. These models were produced in European and US versions until late-1976 (US) and mid-1977 (Europe). The replacement models had steel bodies with glass-fibre front and rear valances, but retained the aluminium front lid. Additionally, the removable roof section of the GTS was also moulded in glass-fibre, and was provided with a vinyl cover for protection when stowed behind the seats. The top windscreen rail on the GTS had a

Optional Equipment

308 GTB/S, 308 GTBi/Si & 208 GTB/S
Air conditioning
Metallic paint
Wide wheels
Deep front spoiler
Fog lights
Pirelli P7 tyres with 16in wheels
'Boxer' paint finish

308 QV & 208 Turbo
Air conditioning
Metallic paint
Deep front spoiler
Pirelli P7 tyres with 16in wheels
Rear aerofoil (standard for Japan and on Turbo)

328 GTB/S & GTB/S Turbo
Air conditioning
Metallic paint
Pirelli P7 tyres
Leather dashboard
Leather headlining plus rear window surround
ABS brakes
Rear aerofoil (standard for Japan and on Turbo)

Note These are the items generally regarded as optional equipment, although in some markets some of them may have been provided as standard. In addition, ranges of Schedoni fitted luggage in leather were available for all models.

Aerial view of 328 GTS illustrates clean lines of final evolution of series, particularly with normally black rear spoiler painted body colour. Scuderia Ferrari shields on front wings are owner's personal addition – these emblems were normally reserved for racing models.

Ferrari
N371
PRINCIPAUTE DE MONACO
MC
328
GTS

concave, curved profile to deflect air over the cabin when the roof was removed.

Air from the front-mounted radiator was expelled through body-coloured, louvred vents behind the retractable headlight pods in the wings. The rear lid contained a pair of louvred vents that ran the length of the engine bay, either side of the central section, these having a matt black paint finish. From the middle of 1977 an optional front valance, incorporating a deep spoiler, became available as a factory-fitted option; as with the standard valance, this was made of glass-fibre.

US models can be easily recognised by their heavier, more protuberant bumpers front and rear, although these were far less cumbersome than those on the 308 GT4. Other distinguishing features were a louvred exhaust shield beneath the rear valance, a four tail-pipe exhaust system (as opposed to the single outlet on European models), and slim, rectangular side marker lights on the front and rear wings. Towards the end of production of the US carburettor version, the rearmost five rows of engine lid louvres were joined across the centre section, to aid heat dissipation, and this feature continued on US fuel-injected models.

Although there were changes to the interior and the wheel design when the fuel-injected models, the 308 GTBi and GTSi, were announced in late 1980, bodily the only difference was the deletion of the cut-out in the rear valance for the single exhaust pipe on European versions, now that they also had a quad-outlet exhaust. Italian market 208 GTB/S models were bodily identical to the normal European models, apart from the front wing louvres being painted matt black instead of body colour.

The QV models featured a revised front grille arrangement, incorporating rectangular driving lights which doubled as daylight headlight flashers. There was also an additional louvred slot in the front lid to aid hot air exit from the radiator. On European versions the front lid and wing louvres were body colour, but for US models and 208 Turbos they were painted matt black. The 208 Turbos had a NACA duct on the lower flank forward of the rear wheel arch, and the deep front spoiler and rear roof spoiler – optional in other markets – were standard on this model. The 208 Turbo front spoiler featured a horizontal row of five slim slots below the grille opening.

Up to this time only a driver's door mirror had been fitted as standard, but the new range featured paired door mirrors, still matt black, but rectangular with a small enamel Ferrari shield on the shroud body. US models had less aerodynamic, larger, rectangular door mirrors, without the enamel shield.

An important development took place in January 1984, as all models produced from that date were manufactured from Zincrox-coated steel panels on internal surfaces most exposed to corrosive action. The Zincrox treatment was an electrolytic-applied, multi-layer coating, comprising a layer of zinc on the steel surface, then a layer of chrome, and finally a layer of chrome oxide. Thus late-model 308 QVs and 208 Turbos, plus all 328 models and GTB/S Turbos, benefited from this treatment.

At the Frankfurt Salon in 1985, ten years after its introduction, the 308 series evolved into the 328 series, with the only body shape change of any note during the production period. The front and rear body sections, from the bumper downwards, were completely redesigned by Pininfarina to soften the wedge effect.

The bumpers had a more rounded, neater profile, while the front side/turn lights moved from the bumper into unit with the driving lights at the grille extremities. The lower section of the front valance acted as a spoiler, and was painted matt black. This matt black finish continued in a straight line along the lower body sides into the rear valance, which was extended down to form a silencer cover on models for all markets.

The louvred radiator outlets behind the retractable headlight pods disappeared and the louvred outlet on the front lid was enlarged to compensate. The engine cover louvre pattern became standard for all markets,

Two Italian market 208 Turbo models serve to illustrate visual differences compared with 3-litre counterparts. Visible on GTB, seen from front, are matt black radiator outlet louvres, low-set NACA duct in front of rear wheel arch, and row of five slots below front grille to direct more air to radiator. On GTS, seen from rear, note air outlet slots in rear bumper and – just visible on engine lid – raised, black-louvred centre section required to clear intercooler.

High 328 GTS view from front shows revised pattern of air extraction louvres, with large panel of them on the front lid but none behind headlight pods.

A non-ABS 328 GTB, immediately identifiable by concave wheel centres. Change to body colour bumpers with altered lower tail panel modernised lines.

with the rearmost five rows extending across the width. A rear roof aerofoil was available as an option on both 328 GTB and GTS models. The new models also featured a revised door catch arrangement, the previous small black lever protruding from the top rear edge of the door being replaced by a flap-type lever in the top face of the door.

European and US 328 models retained the door mirror differences found on the 308 QV series, but this detail was now one of very few ways to tell European and US versions apart – side marker lights and different lamp lens colours were the only other distinguishing features of US models. Throughout the series a single towing eye was provided, mounted on the front right-hand side of the chassis.

In 1986 a version was announced for the Italian market, labelled simply as the GTB or GTS Turbo. As with the previous turbocharged model, there was a NACA duct on each lower body side, forward of the rear wheel arch. The centre section of the engine lid was louvred, and raised to accommodate the inter-cooler. The optional rear roof aerofoil of the 328 was standard, and the rear bumper had five exhaust slots along its length.

DIMENSIONS & WEIGHTS

	Europe	US
208 & 308 series		
Overall length	4230mm (166.5in)	4380mm (172.4in)[1]
Overall width	1720mm (67.7in)	1720mm (67.7in)
Overall height	1120mm (44.1in)	1120mm (44.1in)
Wheelbase	2340mm (92.1in)	2340mm (92.1in)
Front track	1460mm (57.5in)	1460mm (57.5in)
Rear track	1460mm (57.5in)	1460mm (57.5in)
Luggage compartment	245 litres	150 litres
Dry weight		
308 GTB	1330kg (2932lb)	1433kg (3159lb)
308 GTS	1360kg (2998lb)	1463kg (3225lb)
308 GTBi	1341kg (2956lb)	1505kg (3317lb)
308 GTSi	1352kg (2980lb)	1527kg (3366lb)
308 GTB QV	1330kg (2932lb)	1447kg (3190lb)
308 GTS QV	1341kg (2956lb)	1465kg (3229lb)
208 GTB	1305kg (2876lb)	–
208 GTS	1365kg (3009lb)	–
208 GTB Turbo	1284kg (2830lb)	–
208 GTS Turbo	1295kg (2854lb)	–

[1]Overall length of US GTBi/Si and QV is 4425mm (174.2in).

	Europe	US
328 series & GTB/S Turbo		
Overall length	4255mm (167.5in)	4285mm (168.7in)
Overall width	1730mm (68.1in)	1730mm (68.1in)
Overall height	1128mm (44.4in)	1128mm (44.4in)
Wheelbase	2350mm (92.5in)	2350mm (92.5in)
Front track	1485mm (58.5in)	1473mm (57.9in)
Rear track	1465mm (57.7in)	1468mm (57.7in)
Dry weight		
GTB	1263kg (2784lb)	1422kg (3134lb)
GTS	1273kg (2806lb)	1435kg (3163lb)
B Turbo	1265kg (2788lb)	–
S Turbo	1275kg (2810lb)	–

BODY TRIM & FITTINGS

There was virtually no brightwork on the range from inception to demise. All window surrounds were either black rubber or matt black painted metal. The only chrome was on the lock barrels and the *Cavallino*

A 328 GTS ABS version, which can be identified by the Mondial-like convex wheel centres. The lower body panel changes are much more noticeable in this front three-quarter view, where the body colour bumper and a new smoother, deeper, integrated grille and light assembly loses much of the sharp wedge shape that was starting to go out of vogue by the mid-1980s. The family resemblance to the Mondial was also forged by this change.

Rampante badge, which appeared on the tail panel of all models and also on the grille of QVs and 328s.

Tinted glass was standard throughout the life of the series, the windscreen featuring a heavily tinted green band across its top edge. The door windows on all models were electrically operated. Up to and including the 308 QV models, there was a small, circular, removable plug in the interior door panels, to effect manual operation via a crank handle in the event of motor failure. Windscreen wipers, which were finished in matt black, parked on the right for left-hand drive and on the left for right-hand drive.

On the 308 GTB and GTS carburettor cars a single Vitaloni 'California' mirror in matt black plastic was fitted to the driver's door, although a matching passenger-side mirror was available as an option, and frequently fitted. On the 308 GTBi and GTSi, the fuel-injected cars, a single electrically operated door mirror was fitted on the driver's side, rectangular on European models and oval on US versions. The 308 QV, 328 series and Italian Turbo variants had paired electrically operated door mirrors; the European mirrors were a shallow-section rectangle in shape with a curved, black plastic shroud featuring an enamel Ferrari badge, while the US mirrors were deeper rectangles with a flat shroud, and no badge.

The bumpers on all models up to and including the 308 QV were finished in matt black with no brightwork, while those on the 328 and GTB/S Turbo were body colour. US versions up to and including the 308 QV had bumpers of heavier section than their European counterparts, mounted on impact absorbers to comply with US legislation. Although they projected further than the European ones, these

Windscreen pillar detail shows indent line that was unique to glass-fibre versions; glass-fibre mouldings were of such high quality that it is otherwise very difficult, without magnet to hand, to distinguish early 308 GTBs externally from later steel-bodied versions. With rear lid open, however, one can see glass-fibre construction on rear screen surround, and aluminium foil firewall sheeting.

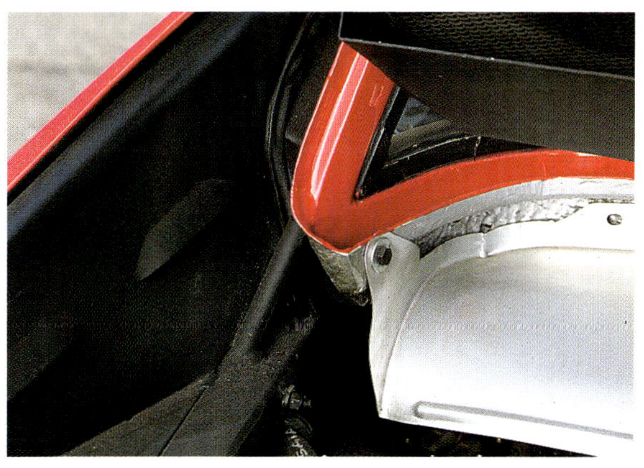

Optional matt black rear spoiler, mounted on engine cover buttresses, had a lightly grained finish (far left). Standard 'targa' roof panel (left) with black vinyl finish that was common to all GTS versions. When removed, roof is stowed behind front seats.

Door handles differed on 308 (far left) and 328 (left). Tapered ducts feed air to engine compartment, and badges recognise design role of Pininfarina. The internal mechanism of this flap type lever was changed twice during the production life of the 328, the first from chassis number 71597, where there was no external difference, and then again from chassis number 75929, which can be identified by a thin black neoprene surround to the pull flap.

Rear quarter window arrangements on GTB (far left) and GTS (left) models, unchanged for duration of range. Only GTS versions had louvred panel over complete quarter window; this was hinged on both sides to permit cleaning of glass, whereas smaller louvred section on GTB models was hinged only on left-hand side to give access to fuel filler.

bumpers were a much more elegant proposition than those fitted to the US-market 308 GT4. Bumper material was moulded glass-fibre on European cars or high-density rubber on a steel backing plate on US versions. On all models up to and including the 308 QV, the front bumpers incorporated the side/turn lights, while European glass-fibre cars also had rectangular reversing lights in the rear bumper.

An enamel rectangular Ferrari badge was fixed by bolted pins into a recess in the nose panel. The model designation badges were in aluminium, on the tail panel between the number plate and right-hand lights, with a chromed *Cavallino Rampante* in a similar position to the left of the number plate. A rectangular 'Disegno di Pininfarina' badge in aluminium featured on the left-hand side of the car, in most cases on the lower body between the trailing edge of the door and the rear wheel arch. The exceptions were the 208 Turbo and GTB/S Turbo models, which had a NACA duct in this position, so on these models the badge appeared above the body crease line behind the rear wheel arch.

The front radiator grille throughout the series was manufactured from plain aluminium formed in an egg-crate pattern. On all European 308 models the grille had a natural finish, but it was painted matt black on US 308s (up to and including the QV) and Italian market 208s and 208 Turbos. This distinction disappeared with the 328s and GTB/S Turbos, these cars having plain aluminium grilles for all markets.

Access to the front boot compartment was via a vertical lever mounted in the cabin on the driver's side wheel arch, while access to the rear engine/boot compartments was via a lockable lever in the driver's door shut post. Emergency pull rings were also provided, should the cable fail on the primary release.

Italian market Turbo details (facing page): quarter bumpers and shrouded exhaust tailpipes were unique to 208 Turbo, while extra NACA duct ahead of each rear wheel – seen on GTS Turbo – was present on all 'blown' models.

Various bonnet and front wing louvre arrangements through life span of range: 308 (upper left), 308 QV (centre), 328 (right) and 208 Turbo (lower left).

Complex evolution of tail badging! On all models except 308 QV and 208 Turbo, lettering signified whether a car was a Berlinetta (GTB) or Spider (GTS).

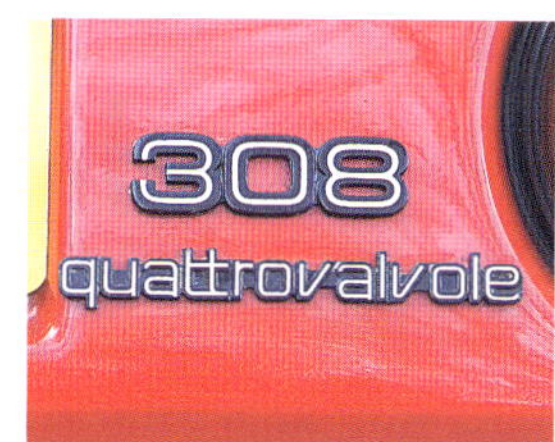

The 308 GTB/S interior has fairly plain leather seat panels, and finish of solid steering wheel spokes is natural aluminium.

The fuel filler on closed cars was mounted behind a small, lockable, hinged panel at the rear of the left-hand rear quarter glass. The position was the same on targa-roofed cars, but on these the complete louvred screen covering the quarter glass was hinged and lockable. The filler fed into the left-hand tank of the twin-tank installation, and across to the right-hand tank via the tank balance pipe. A small plastic flap folded out from the filler aperture to protect the paintwork from the pump nozzle or petrol spillage.

Paintwork

For the first five years of production, that is to say for the carburettor models, the paint used was acrylic produced by Glidden Salchi of Milan, comprising 11 solid colours and 10 two-pack metallic finishes. From 1980 the paint manufacturer was Glasurit, and the range of colours available changed over the production period of the cars. Paint colours and codes are listed in the accompanying panel.

'Boxer' paint finish was available as an optional extra until the end of the GTBi/GTSi period. This involved painting the lower body half matt black, up to the normally black-painted indent line.

Interior Trim & Fittings

The 308 GTB/S seats were trimmed in leather, featured side bolsters on squab and backrest to improve lateral support, and matching head restraints were fitted. Mounted on runners for fore/aft adjustment, the seats also had adjustable backrests, controlled manually by a knob on the outside lower end of the backrest. A backrest release lever was provided adjacent to the knob, to allow it to tilt forward for access to the slim space behind the seats.

The dashboard was finished in black vinyl, the line of the ends being carried diagonally down the door panels to form door pulls/armrests. The door release catch was mounted in the lower edge of the armrest and the electric window switches in the top. As on the 308 GT4, a removable plug was provided in the door panels to permit manual operation of the windows via a crank handle if the motor failed. Below the armrests were matching black door pockets that incorporated radio speakers at the forward end. The main door panel was trimmed in the same colour as the seats. Small, circular 'door open' warning lights were located in the trailing edge of the doors.

Body Colours

1975-79 MODEL YEARS	
Solid colours	**Code**
Rosso Chiaro	20.3.90
Rosso Dino	20.3.350
Blu Scurro Dino	20.A.357
Azzurro Dino	20.A.349
Verde Germolgio	20.G.465
Giallo Senappe	20.Y.464
Nuovo Giallo Fly	20.Y.490
Giallo Dino	20.Y.348
Bianco Polo Park	20.W.152
Nero	N/A
Bleu Montecarlo	N/A
Metallic colours	
Verde Pino	N/A
Verde Medio	N/A
Blu Dino	N/A
Blu Sera	N/A
Azzurro Metalizzato	N/A
Marrone Dino	N/A
Grigio Ferro	N/A
Oro Chiaro	N/A
Argento Auteil	N/A
Rosso Rubino	N/A

1980-83 MODEL YEARS	
Solid colours	**Code**
Bianco	FER 100
Giallo	FER 102
Rosso Corsa	FER 300
Rosso Dino	FER 301
Azzurro	FER 500
Blu Scuro	FER 501
Nero	FER 1240
Metallic colours	
Argento	101/C
Oro Chiaro	103/C
Rosso	302/C
Marrone	303/C
Azzurro	502/C
Blu Chiaro	503/C
Blu Sera	504/C
Verde Medio	600/C
Verde Pino	601/C
Grigio	700/C

1984-89 MODEL YEARS	
Solid colours	**Code**
Bianco	FER 100
Giallo	FER 102
Rosso Corsa	FER 300/6
Nero	FER 1240
Metallic colours	
Argento	101/C
Oro Chiaro	104/C
Rosso	305/C
Prugna	306/C
Blu Chiaro	503/C
Blu Sera	504/C
Azzurro	505/C
Blu Medio	506/C
Verde Chiaro	602/C
Verde Scuro	603/C
Verde Tenue	604/C
Grigio	700/C
Marrone	800/C
Nero	901/C

Notes Optional 'Boxer' colour scheme, available 1975-82, had matt black lower body (code 20.B.50 plus 20.T.380 matt lacquer). From January 1989 metallic colour codes gained an FER prefix.

For 308 GTBi/Si, seat panels have rib-effect pattern stitched into them, and steering wheel spokes have become matt black with longitudinal slots.

On the GTS the roof was secured via two retaining catches on the roll-over hoop and locating pins in the trailing edge of the windscreen rail. It was provided with a black vinyl protective bag for stowage vertically behind the seats. The GTB model had a glovebox at the rear of the central tunnel between the seats, but this was omitted on the GTS model to permit roof storage. On the GTS the driver's door pocket was also substituted for a flexible document pocket with cover flap retained by a stud fastener.

The floor, sills, inner front wheel arches and rear wall were carpeted, and the driver's mat featured a black rubber heel pad. The roof lining was an open-weave cream cloth that extended down the rear pillars to form a surround to the rear screen.

Driver and passenger sun visors were provided, the passenger one incorporating a vanity mirror. The interior rear-view mirror was of the dipping variety, attached to the screen by an adhesive pad. In the GTB the interior light was in the centre rear of the roof, while in the GTS it was mounted between the sun visors on the windscreen rail. The glovebox on the GTB was also provided with a light.

The central tunnel between the seats housed the open-gate gear change at the forward end. Behind the gear lever was a chromed *Cavallino Rampante* and there was an ashtray alongside this. From here the tunnel sloped rearwards to a lower level, with a cigarette lighter and air conditioning controls (where fitted) on the slope. The flat rear section featured a row of black-handled lever switches for fan, hazard warning lights and wiper speed. Next to these was a small chrome switch for the rear wing-mounted electric aerial. The aerial and door-mounted twin speaker installation were standard, although a radio was an option. Behind this row of switches were levers in slots controlling air flow to driver's side, heater output, air flow to passenger's side and choke. The final item on the tunnel was the handbrake, which had a chrome lever and ribbed black plastic handle, and, on the GTB only, protruded from the curved front face of the glovebox.

The steering wheel was a Momo with three plain spokes in aluminium, a leather-covered rim, and a central horn push bearing the *Cavallino Rampante* on a yellow background.

When the 308 GTBi/Si fuel-injected models were announced, changes were made to the interior trim and fittings. The seat panel design was changed, with the new stitching providing a fishbone effect on the

Leather Upholstery Colours

Colour	Code
Grigio	VM 3393
Nero	VM 8500
Beige	VM 4208
Crema	VM 3997
Rosso	VM 3171
Blu	VM 3282

The 308 QV interior did not alter tremendously from its predecessor, although cloth seat centres could be specified and steering wheel design changed again.

squab and backrest central panels. The door panel design was altered relative to the door pockets, which became carpet-faced with a cut-out for the radio speakers near the front edge.

The steering wheel spokes gained longitudinal slots and were painted matt black to match the revised finish for the instrument panel. The centre console design was altered in front of the gear lever to house the relocated clock and oil temperature gauge, and an oddments tray was sited in front of them. The chrome *Cavallino Rampante* moved from behind the gear-shift gate to the lid of the ashtray, its old position being used for the electric window switches, moved from the armrests. The electric aerial switch received a lever to match the design of the others on the console. The fuse/relay board cover on the passenger side of the dashboard received a chrome GTBi or GTSi badge.

When the Quattrovalvole models were introduced, a few further alterations occurred to the interior details. The driver's door pull/armrest incorporated control toggles for the new electric door mirrors. The steering wheel design was amended to a matt black dished style, with a large, almost triangular surround to the horn button, and the leather of the rim was extended along the matt black spokes (which were once again of plain design) towards the hub section. The roof lining became a fine beige/brown or black/grey striped cloth, depending upon the interior colour scheme. On the GTB model the interior roof light moved into a new roof console and incorporated a directional movement facility.

When the 328 models were introduced, the interior was once again remodelled to reflect the external changes. The seat panel stitch pattern was altered to create a series of rectangles, although the overall profile remained virtually unchanged. The door panel was redesigned to provide a separate armrest and door pull; the armrest was finished in the interior colour, while the door pull section was black to match the dashboard from which it extended. There was also an elasticated pocket below the armrest, integral with the trapezoidal shape, and the front bottom corner of the panel, up to the door pull, was carpet-faced. The electric window switches moved from the centre console to the redesigned door pulls, which incorporated courtesy lights and initially the door release catch. In mid-1988 this catch was moved to the front corner of the armrest – the only change to the interior during the 328 production run. The driver's side door pull also housed the external mirror adjustment switches.

Carpet Colours

Colour	Code
Nero	80
Rosso	81
Testa di Moro	83
Blu	84
Bruciato	85

The 328 GTB/S saw extensive interior changes, almost everything being redesigned and modernised in keeping with exterior updates. Most obvious differences are again to seat stitch pattern, minor instruments and steering wheel, but note door pulls and switchgear too.

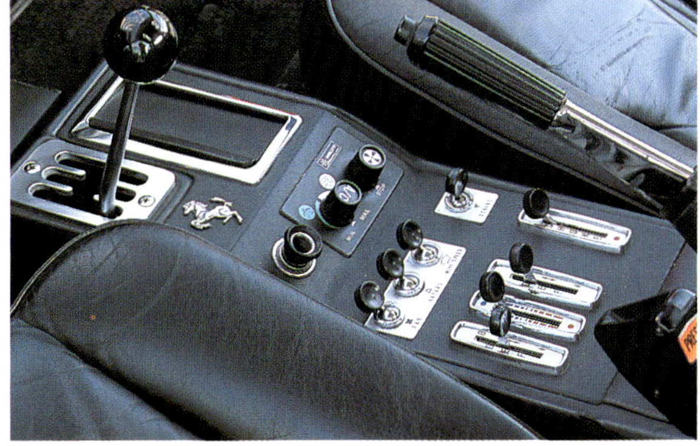

Centre console design went through four basic variants (from top left): 308 GTB/S, 308 GTBi/Si, 308 QV and 328 GTB/S.

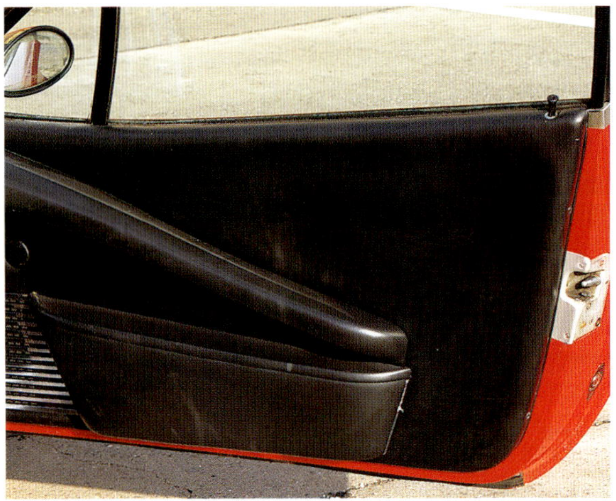

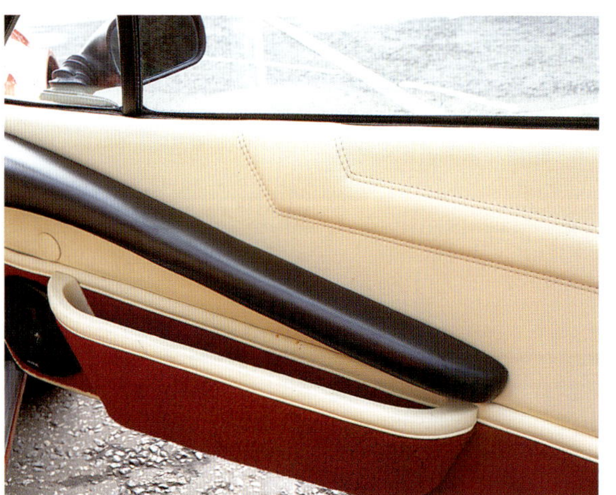

Variations in door panel design during life span of these models. General design was unchanged through 308 series, although details differed: 308 GTB (far left) and 308 QV (left) are shown for comparison. Significant redesign occurred for introduction of 328 (below left), with different layout for armrest, pocket, pull and catch.

Catch moved from within door pull to armrest (above) when ABS became standard on 328 models in 1988. The armrest also became black with the introduction of ABS as standard.

As with its predecessors, the gearchange gate was on the driver's side of the tunnel, with the ashtray alongside it. However, to the rear the switchgear was completely redesigned to incorporate more modern units, and the handbrake was moved to the outside of the driver's seat, thus enabling a lockable glovebox to be provided between the seats on both GTB and GTS variants, although the GTS had a shallower one.

The supplementary instruments were moved from the centre console to a new centre panel on the dashboard, and this also incorporated two directional air vents on the lower section of the face, with space for a radio installation above. The dashboard badge became GTB or GTS, dependant upon model.

As an option, a full leather interior became available on this model, so that the roof lining plus rear window surround covering could be ordered as one option, and a full leather dash as another. Although any colour could be specified, it was always recommended that the dash be left in black to minimise reflections in the windscreen.

The Italian-market 208 GTB/S, 208 Turbo and GTB/S Turbo models had interiors very similar to the main world-market models, although the 208-designated models had cloth centre seats as standard, and the Turbos had a 'turbo' script on the dashboard in addition to a boost gauge on the instrument panel.

DASHBOARD & INSTRUMENTS

The dashboard was a simple design, forming a sloping flat panel rolling over into the fuse/relay board cover on the passenger side, with a deep, hooded, trapezoidal instrument nacelle directly in front of the driver. The instrument panel within the nacelle had a brushed aluminium finish on the 308 GTB/S models, but from the 308 GTBi/Si onwards it was painted matt black.

Within the nacelle were the speedometer (incorporating distance recorder and trip meter) and rev counter, and between them was an inverted triangle of dials comprising an oil pressure gauge placed centrally at the bottom and fuel and water temperature gauges above. The trip control and instrument light rheostat knobs were below the oil pressure gauge, with four warning lights completing the panel.

All US models also had a 'fasten seat belts' warning light below the oil pressure gauge. On US models with catalytic converters there were further warning lights, on the lower dash either side of the steering column, stating 'Slow down cyl 1-4' and 'Slow down cyl 5-8' if the catalytic converter was overheating.

Initially there was a separate console between the steering column and door post to house the clock and oil temperature gauge, barely visible from the driver's seat. On the GTBi/Si and Quattrovalvole models these two gauges were moved to a nacelle on the centre console. With the introduction of the 328, the clock, oil temperature and fuel gauges were sited on the dashboard face in a centre panel. The water temperature gauge moved to the former position of the oil pressure gauge in the main panel, with the latter now positioned immediately above it. On the 208 Turbo model, the boost gauge replaced the clock in the centre console, while on the GTB/S Turbo it was mounted in the centre of the main panel, with the oil pressure and water temperature gauges above it, forming an inverted triangle.

All dials were coloured white-on-black up to and including the Quattrovalvole models, but the 328 models changed to orange-on-black. The speedometer read to 180mph or 280kph on all models, apart from an exception in the US where, due to legislation introduced in 1979, some cars were fitted with speedometers that read only to 85mph; this requirement was rescinded in mid-1982, although many cars had already been retro-fitted with 'normal'

Detail of pre-ABS 328 door pull on driver's side, showing electric window switches.

Instrument panel in 308 GTB/S carburettor models featured plain aluminium face; clock and oil temperature gauge (top right) were housed in supplementary panel between steering column and door.

The 328 (below) had a more rounded instrument nacelle and orange markings on dials; fuel gauge moved to join clock and oil temperature gauge (below right) in new console in dashboard centre.

The 308 GTBi/Si and QV instrument panel (left) was similar in layout to carburettor cars, but had matt black face – and supplementary pair of dials moved to more easily visible location on leading edge of centre console. For right-hand drive, rev counter and speedometer (reading to 180mph instead of 280kph) changed places.

The 208 Turbo centre console (right), with boost gauge forward of gearchange. Later GTB/S Turbo (far right), unlike parallel 328 models, retained three small dials in instrument panel so that boost gauge could be accommodated, but shared central bank of three dials with its normally aspirated sisters.

speedometers. The rev counter, which always read to 10,000rpm, had yellow figures from 7000rpm and red from 7700rpm on all models up to and including the Quattrovalvole, but on the 328 there was simply a red line at 7800rpm.

To the left of the steering column were two stalks, the shorter actuating the direction indicators and the longer the lighting functions. To the right of the column was another stalk for windscreen wipers and washers. Although the detail design of these stalks changed through the various models, their functions remained the same.

Three circular demisting outlets with directional flaps were located in the top centre of the dashboard, and a further two slots were provided at the top front corners of the dashboard. Up to and including the Quattrovalvole models, two rectangular directional vents were mounted below the centre of the dashboard, but on the 328 models these were incorporated into the new centre console.

The centre tunnel console contained the gear lever in an open gate on all models. Behind this were the air conditioning controls (where fitted) and then, on all models up to and including the Quattrovalvole, a bank of four switches which controlled (from left) ventilation fan, hazard warning lights, wiper speed and electric aerial. Behind these were four levers in longitudinal slots, the first three controlling (from left) left-hand side air flow, heater output and right-hand side airflow. The fourth lever controlled the choke on 308 GTB/S models, but for the fuel-injected 308 GTBi/Si and Quattrovalvole, which had no choke function, the redundant lever was used to improve heat distribution by allowing separate heat control as well as ventilation fan control to both sides of the passenger compartment. The handbrake was to the rear of this arrangement.

For the 328 models the centre console was considerably updated, and the handbrake moved to the outside of the driver's seat. Behind the gear lever on a sloping panel were controls for the air conditioning (where fitted), with two circular rotating knobs for temperature (left) and output (right), and a cigarette lighter to the right of these. On the horizontal section behind followed a bank of three controls comprising left-hand ventilation fan control knob, hazard warning light push button and right-hand ventilation fan control knob. Behind these were four switches for (from left) left-hand air flow direction, left-hand heat output, right-hand heat output and right-hand air flow direction.

The rearmost bank of push buttons on 328s were for various functions, according to market. The left-hand switch on standard European cars was either a 'dummy' (left-hand drive) or operated the front fog lights (right-hand drive), while for US models it operated the heated rear window. The next switch was for rear fog lights except in the case of US and South African cars, on which it operated the front fog lights. The other two switches, for all markets, operated the radio aerial and parking lights.

LUGGAGE COMPARTMENT

The main luggage space on all models was at the rear of the car in a rectangular compartment under the main engine cover lid. This was carpeted and provided with a black vinyl zipped cover to protect the contents. With the silencer assembly immediately below the compartment and the engine in front of it, care has to be taken not to stow anything that might be affected by heat...

Further stowage space for flat items was available behind the seats, although on GTS models this space is occupied by the roof panel when removed. Small, soft bags can be accommodated around the spare wheel under the front lid, although care has to be taken not to force the lid closed on bulky items, as it could become distorted.

Rear luggage compartment of 308, showing protective zipped cover that remained basically unchanged throughout life of series. Front compartment of 308 GTB, with zipped cover over spacesaver spare wheel. US market cars had to carry full-size spare, which was a tight fit. For 308 QV, minor front compartment changes were required to accommodate front lid radiator outlet louvres. Wheel well was deepened to accommodate full-size spare more easily, and there was no zipped cover.

TOOL KIT

Tool roll
- Carburettor spanner (308 GTB/S & 208 GTB/S only)
- Range of eight open-end spanners, 6-22mm
- Pliers, 180mm long
- Flat-blade screwdriver, 120mm long
- Flat-blade screwdriver, 150mm long
- Phillips screwdriver, 4mm diameter
- Phillips screwdriver, 5-9mm diameter
- Spark plug spanner
- Exhaust gas analyser extension tubes (US & Australia)

Tool bag
- Scissor-type jack with ratchet drive
- Wheel nut spanner
- Alternator belt
- Air conditioner compressor belt (where fitted)
- Air pump control belts (US & Australia)
- Emergency hazard warning triangle (EU)
- Set of fuses
- Set of bulbs
- Sparking plugs (2)

Carburettor 308 GTB/S engine compartment looks little different from that of 308 GT4, with air filter prominent.

The rear lid was released by a chromed lever in the driver's door shut post, supplemented by an emergency ring pull on the rear bulkhead in case of failure of the primary system. The front lid had a similar lever on the front wheel arch on the driver's side, again with an emergency ring pull mounted just above it, below the dash panel.

The front compartment also housed the battery in a covered well below the spare wheel, the left and right ventilation fans in the respective lower front wing corners, the air horns, the brake master cylinder and reservoir, and the windscreen washer bottle, under a plastic shroud. Initially the spare wheel in the front compartment was protected by a zipped cover, but this was dispensed with for the Quattrovalvole and 328 models.

Each car came with a comprehensive tool kit and certain spares supplied in a roll and a bag in soft vinyl. On European 308 GTB/S, 308 GTBi/Si and Italian 208 GTB/S cars the roll and bag were sited in the spare wheel well on top of the spacesaver tyre, but subsequent models – and all US versions – had them fixed in the boot. The range of tools and spares provided was generally as listed in the panel.

Engine

The basic engine configuration of the 308 GTB/S was exactly the same as on the 308 GT4 models, being a 90° V8 of 2926cc (178.6cu in) with bore and stroke of 81mm (3.19in) by 71mm (2.79in). However, it was given the type code F106AB in carburettor form and adapted to dry-sump lubrication for European markets, although cars for the US, Japan and Australia initially retained the GT4's wet-sump system as well as its twin distributor ignition system. Japanese engines had type code F106AE, also given to US models from 1978.

The dry-sump lubrication system pressurised the engine via a geared pump, with a further two pumps that sucked oil from the sump, passed it through a cooling radiator in the engine compartment and then to the collector tank, from where it was sucked back to the engine by the initial pump. The collector tank cap had a built-in dipstick for checking oil level.

As with the 308 GT4, quoted power figures varied from market to market according to the emission control equipment fitted. As an example, the European models were initially quoted at 255bhp, US and Australian models at 240bhp. By 1980 the European figure had dropped to 230bhp and the US figure to 205bhp. When fuel injection and electronic ignition were introduced to the range in late 1980 and the model designation received the 'i' suffix, output fell even further to 214bhp on European models, although US engines remained quoted at 205bhp.

Fuel-injected models can easily be identified by the cast aluminium intake box on top of the engine, instead of the black air filter box of carburettor cars. The engine code became F106BB and at the same

Fuel injection 308 GTBi/Si engine compartment (above), with cast alloy injection intake box replacing sheet steel air filter. The 308 QV engine compartment (facing page) received attractive red crackle finish to injection intake casting, with raised ribbing and lettering.

time wet-sump lubrication was standardised for all world markets.

The Bosch K Jetronic injection system delivered fuel to the engine via a high-pressure electric pump through a fuel accumulator, filter and mixture control unit, and thence via individual pipes to the cylinder injection nozzles. The electronic ignition system was a Marelli MED 803A Digiplex unit that incorporated a coil, distributor head and electronic ignition module to serve each bank of cylinders. A diagnostic socket was located on the left of the engine compartment, to enable the system to be plugged into diagnostic equipment to check that it was functioning correctly.

In late 1982 steps were taken to redress the fall in power output with the introduction of four-valves-per-cylinder heads, together with Nikasil-faced cylinder liners instead of cast iron ones, and the adoption of flat-top pistons. The result of these modifications boosted the power of European models to a quoted 235-240bhp, and US models to 230-235bhp. The injection intake box above the engine vee became a more elegant casting, finished in red crackle paint and with raised, polished ribs bearing the Ferrari script and Quattrovalvole legend.

For an as-yet unknown reason, the engine family type code for US versions was referred to in the owner's handbook for 1983 as DFE179V6G4V6 and for 1984 as EFE179V6F4V4, the former quoting power output at 230bhp and the latter at 235bhp, both at 6800rpm.

The final evolution of the transverse V8 engine came when it was enlarged to 3185cc (194.4cu in) for the introduction of the 328 series in late 1985, pushing up power output at 7000rpm to a quoted 270bhp for European models and 260bhp for US models. The capacity increase was achieved by enlarging both bore and stroke by 2mm, giving dimensions of 83mm (3.27in) by 73mm (2.87in). There were also revised inlet camshafts with higher lift, redesigned piston heads and smaller 12mm spark plugs. The Marelli electronic ignition system changed from Digiplex to the more compact and versatile MED 806A Microplex system, featuring a single electronic ignition module for both banks while still retaining a coil and distributor head for each bank. The system diagnostic socket remained on the left-hand side of the engine bay. The injection intake box was further modified, becoming an even more elegant unit in plain aluminium with red infill between the ribbing on the top face.

The 1991cc (121.5cu in) Italian market engine, type code F106CB, was essentially a small-bore

TIMING DATA

308 GTB/S	Single distributor	Twin distributor
Inlet opens BTDC	30°	34°
Inlet closes ABDC	50°	46°
Exhaust opens BBDC	36°	36°
Exhaust closes ATDC	28°	38°

308 GTBi/Si	Electronic ignition (EU)	(US)
Inlet opens BTDC	16°	16°
Inlet closes ABDC	48°	48°
Exhaust opens BBDC	54°	50°
Exhaust closes ATDC	10°	14°

208 GTB/S	Single distributor
Inlet opens BTDC	22°
Inlet closes ABDC	42°
Exhaust opens BBDC	40°
Exhaust closes ATDC	24°

208 TURBO	Electronic ignition
Inlet opens BTDC	20°
Inlet closes ABDC	44°
Exhaust opens BBDC	54°
Exhaust closes ATDC	10°

GTB/S TURBO	Electronic ignition
Inlet opens BTDC	18°
Inlet closes ABDC	46°
Exhaust opens BBDC	54°
Exhaust closes ATDC	10°

308 GTB/S QV	Electronic ignition (EU)	(US)
Inlet opens BTDC	16°	16°
Inlet closes ABDC	48°	48°
Exhaust opens BBDC	54°	40°
Exhaust closes ATDC	10°	14°

328 GTB/S	Electronic ignition (EU & USA)
Inlet opens BTDC	16°
Inlet closes ABDC	48°
Exhaust opens BBDC	54°
Exhaust closes ATDC	10°

Valve timing should be measured with a clearance of 0.50mm (0.020in) between the tappet thimbles and camshaft. Valve clearances with cold engine should be 0.20-0.25mm (0.008-0.010in) for inlet valves, 0.30-0.35mm (0.012-0.014in) for exhaust valves on two-valve engines or 0.35-0.40mm (0.014-0.016in) for exhaust valves on four-valve engines, measured between the valve pads and camshaft. Firing order is 1-5-3-7-4-8-2-6.

version of the 308 unit, with the bore reduced to 66.8mm (2.63in), and it also had wet-sump lubrication. The naturally aspirated 208 GTB/S models of 1980-82 had a quoted power output of 155bhp at 6800rpm. With four Weber 34 DCNF carburettors, these were the last Ferraris to be produced with carburettor engines.

In 1982 the 208 Turbo was introduced, with a single KKK turbocharger operating at 0.6 bar and compression ratio reduced from 9:1 to 7:1, resulting in increased power output of 220bhp at 7000rpm. Concurrently Bosch K-Jetronic fuel injection and Marelli MED 804A Digiplex electronic ignition were introduced, the latter again having a diagnostic check socket on the left-hand side of the engine bay.

The final evolution of the Italian market model was the GTB/S Turbo, introduced in 1986, carrying K-Jetronic injection, an IHI turbocharger with Behr intercooler, and Marelli MED 807A Microplex electronic ignition. It produced 254bhp at 6500rpm, with a compression ratio of 6.5:1 and substantially higher boost pressure of 1.05 bar.

In terms of general construction, layout and locations of ancillaries (such as starter motor, alternator and water pump) the engine was very similar to that described for the 308 GT4, except where noted.

SYSTEM CAPACITIES (LITRES)

Model	Fuel	Cooling	Washer	Engine oil	Gearbox oil
308 GTB/S (dry)	74	18	1	11	4
308 GTB/S (wet)	74	18	2	9	4
308 GTB/S (US)	70	18	2	9	4
308 GTBi/Si	74	18	2	8	4
308 GTBi/Si (US)	70	18	2	8	4
308 QV	74	18	2	10	4
308 QV (US)	70	22	2	10	4
208 GTB/S	74	18	2	9	4
208 Turbo	74	18	2	9	4
328 GTB/S	74	22	3	10	4
GTB/S Turbo	74	22	3	10	4

The four Weber twin-choke carburettors of 308 GTB/S models were 40 DCNF 57-58-59-60 for Europe, 40 DCNF 45-46-47-48 for the US and 40 DCNF 64-65-66-67 for Australia, while for the 208 GTB/S they were 34 DCNF 82-83-84-85. The introduction of fuel injection enabled a standardisation of equipment to Bosch K-Jetronic, which permitted adjustments for various market requirements within a single package. Similarly the adoption of the Marelli Microplex and subsequent Digiplex electronic ignition systems gave greater internal adjustment scope for the various markets, although there remained model differences as previously noted.

Inlet and exhaust valves were inclined with respect to each other at an angle of 46° on two-valve heads or 33° 30′ on four-valve heads, and driven by bucket tappets with spacer shims from their relative camshafts. Valve timing data for all two-valve and four-valve engines is given in the panel on page 51.

All engines were water-cooled via a front-mounted radiator that was fitted with a pair of thermostatically controlled electric fans, circulation being by a belt-driven water pump at the timing gear end of the engine. The cooling system header tank was located in the left-hand rear corner of the engine bay, fitted with a bayonet pressure-relief cap. The heating

The 328 engine compartment featured an even more elaborate and attractive intake unit that sat proudly above the engine. Seen in close-up, it is a fine example of the quality of Ferrari's aluminium casting.

Two phases in Italian market turbocharged engine evolution. For 208 Turbo (1982-85), engine had intake casting and inlet from turbocharger in red crackle finish, with 'turbo' in polished raised lettering on top face. For GTB/S Turbo (1986-89), intercooler with cast aluminium cover and 'turbo' script dominates compartment, dwarfing blue oil filter.

Overall Gear Ratios

308 GTB/S

Gear	Europe	US
First	1:12.669	1:13.303
Second	1:8.719	1:8.719
Third	1:6.274	1:6.274
Fourth	1:4.611	1:4.611
Fifth	1:3.405	1:3.529
Reverse	1:12.036	1:12.036
Final drive	17/63	17/63

308 GTBi/Si

Gear	Europe	US
First	1:13.888	1:13.303
Second	1:9.559	1:8.719
Third	1:6.878	1:6.274
Fourth	1:5.055	1:4.611
Fifth	1:3.736	1:3.529
Reverse	1:13.194	1:12.036
Final drive	16/65	17/63

308 GTB/S QV

Gear	Europe	US	Switzerland
First	1:13.072	1:13.888	1:13.303
Second	1:8.996	1:9.559	1:8.719
Third	1:6.473	1:6.878	1:6.274
Fourth	1:4.756	1:5.055	1:4.611
Fifth	1:3.514	1:3.736	1:3.529
Reverse	1:12.419	1:13.194	1:12.036
Final drive	17/65	16/65	17/63

328 GTB/S

Gear	Europe	US
First	1:12.670	1:13.4259
Second	1:8.719	1:9.2401
Third	1:6.274	1:6.6490
Fourth	1:4.610	1:4.8870
Fifth	1:3.407	1:3.6111
Reverse	1:12.039	1:12.7546
Final drive	17/63	16/65

ITALIAN MARKET

Gear	208 GTB/S	208 Turbo	GTB/S Turbo
First	1:15.722	1:15.479	1:12.670
Second	1:10.823	1:10.146	1:8.719
Third	1:7.787	1:7.301	1:6.274
Fourth	1:5.722	1:5.366	1:4.610
Fifth	1:4.052	1:3.780	1:3.407
Reverse	1:14.936	1:14.005	1:12.039
Final drive	17/63	16/69	17/63

system worked on the same principle as that of the 308 GT4, with separate fans and heater boxes for each side of the passenger compartment. Anti-freeze concentration was specified at approximately one-third for temperatures down to −15° C and half down to −30° C.

The air filter on the intake system was fed via a flexible rubber hose from the right-hand body side intake, while the left-hand body side intake fed air to the oil cooler mounted on that side of the engine bay. The design of these intakes is typical of Pininfarina's ability to combine function with beauty.

European 308 GTB/S models had tubular steel exhaust manifolds to each bank of cylinders, the front bank joining the rear one prior to the system entering the silencer box, which was horizontally suspended below the rear luggage compartment floor. A single tail-pipe with chromed end exited via a cut-out in the panel below the rear bumper. Cars for the US, Japan and Australia had pressed steel manifolds incorporating injection points from the emission control system, and featured two pairs of exhaust tail-pipes. Japanese models were fitted with catalytic converters and a charcoal canister. A 'sports' exhaust system was a factory option for European models, and this featured the now traditional paired twin tail-pipes.

With the introduction of the 308 GTBi/Si injection models, and on all world-market models thereafter, a paired twin tail-pipe arrangement was standard. From the introduction of the QV models, all US cars were fitted with a catalytic converter, which was also adapted for Swiss market cars from 1987, with models for the Austrian and Swedish markets following suit in 1988.

The 208 GTB/S cars had a single tail-pipe, the 208 Turbo paired twin tail-pipes in oval shrouds, and the GTB/S models a standard paired twin tail-pipe arrangement. On the Turbo models the exhaust gases were obviously routed via the turbocharger, which was mounted to the rear of the engine.

TRANSMISSION

The overall transmission assembly for all models was of exactly the same configuration, and manner of operation, as that described for the 308 GT4, being a five-speed gearbox in unit with the engine, clutch and differential assemblies.

Apart from a higher fifth gear, the ratios, including the final drive, were initially taken from the GT4 for European 308 GTB/S models. US versions received a lower first gear and the fifth gear ratio of the GT4. Whereas Australian 308 GT4s had shared the same ratios as the US versions, Australian 308 GTB/S models now had the same ratios as European cars. The Japanese importer modified the clutch mechanisms on cars imported there, in order to meet a lower pedal pressure requirement.

With the introduction of the 308 GTBi/Si models, a forced lubrication system was provided via an output shaft-driven oil pump with small cage-type filter, which together with a change of selector mechanism bearings, from white metal to roller type, was intended to reduce noise and make for a lighter gearchange. Concurrently the clutch-operating mechanism was modified to a simpler arrangement that reduced the required pedal pressure by a third.

The 328 model received a hydraulically operated clutch mechanism, sharing the brake system fluid reservoir. However, the Italian market GTB/S Turbos retained a cable operated clutch.

There were no other major changes to the transmission, although gear and final drive ratios changed from model to model to suit revisions to engine characteristics and road wheel/tyre type. Data for all models and markets is given in the panel on page 53.

Design of pop-up headlight, seen on 328, was unchanged throughout range.

MAJOR ELECTRICAL EQUIPMENT

308 GTB/S	
Battery	12V 60/66Ah
Alternator	Bosch 0.120.489.542
Voltage regulator (in alternator)	Bosch 0.19.20.52.004
Distributor (single, Europe)	Marelli S127G
Distributor (twin, US/AUS)	Marelli S159B
Coils	Marelli BZR201A
Starter motor	Bosch A 001315041
Sparking plugs	Champion N7Y
308 GTBi/Si	
Battery	12V 60/66Ah
Alternator (Europe)	Bosch 65A
Alternator (US)	Bosch A.120.421.251
Voltage regulator (in alternator, US)	Bosch 0.192.052.005
Electronic ignition (Europe)	Marelli MED802A
Electronic ignition (US)	Marelli MED801A
Coils	Marelli BAE209B
Starter motor	Bosch 0.001.314.006
Sparking plugs	Champion N76Y or Bosch W6DS
308 GTB/S QV	
Battery	12V 60/66Ah
Alternator	Bosch 80A
Voltage regulator (in alternator)	N/A
Electronic ignition (EU)	Marelli Digiplex MED 803A
Electronic ignition (US/AUS/CH)	Marelli Digiplex MED 805A
Coils	Marelli BAE 209B
Starter motor	Bosch 0.001.314.006
Sparking plugs	Champion N6GY or RN6GY, Bosch W6DS
328 GTB/S	
Battery	12V 60/66Ah
Alternator	Bosch 85A
Electronic ignition (EU)	Marelli Microplex MED806A
Electronic ignition (US)	Marelli Microplex MED806A
Coils	Marelli AEI500C
Starter motor	Bosch 0.001.110.004
Sparking plugs	Champion A-6G (12mm)
208 GTB/S	
Battery	12V 60/66Ah
Alternator	Bosch 0.120.489.641
Voltage regulator (in alternator)	Bosch 0.19.20.52.005
Distributor	Marelli SM805B
Coils	Marelli AE1200A
Starter motor	Bosch A001315041
Sparking plugs	Champion N7Y
208 Turbo	
Battery	12V 60/66Ah
Alternator	Bosch 65A
Coils	Marelli BAE 209B
Electronic ignition	Marelli Digiplex MED804A
Starter motor	Bosch A001351041
Sparking plugs	Champion N2G
GTB/S Turbo	
Battery	12V 60/66Ah
Alternator	Bosch 70A
Coils	Marelli AEI 500C
Electronic ignition	Marelli Microplex MED807A
Starter motor	Bosch 0.001.110.004
Sparking plugs	Champion N2G

ELECTRICAL EQUIPMENT & LIGHTS

The electrical system was 12-volt, served from a 60Ah or 66Ah battery and fed by a Bosch alternator. Type references for the significant components on the various models are given in the panel.

The specification of the lighting equipment fitted during the life of the series changed not only from model to model, but also according to market destination – but manufacture by Carello remained constant. The headlights, single 7in diameter units, were mounted in the front wings in pods raised by electric motors, which were actuated by relays when the lights were switched on. In case of failure each pod motor had a manual operation facility, via a knurled knob on the end of the motor.

The headlight bulbs were 55 watt main/dipped halogen on European and Australian 308 GTB/S models, but 50 watt on US equivalents. All subsequent European models had 55/60 watt filaments, while US versions continued to differ with 50/60 watt filaments. All French market models had yellow lenses in line with that country's lighting legislation.

All US market cars had orange front side/turn indicator lights, with small rectangular side marker lights surface-mounted on the wings, in amber at the front and red at the rear. European models up to the 308 GTBi/Si had a small, circular, amber indicator repeater light on each front wing just ahead of the wheel arch. On QV models this became a slim rectangular unit in a similar location, while for the 328 a round unit was re-instated but moved to a position between the wheel arch and the door . Cars for Japan varied yet again: 308 GTB/S models had large amber front wing marker lights sourced from Fiat, 308 GTBi/Si models had side marker lights like the US models but these acted as indicator repeaters, while QV and 328 models were fitted with European-specification side indicator lights.

The front side/indicator light lenses of European models were either white or orange/white according to lighting legislation in the country of sale. On the QV models driving lights for daytime flashing were fitted in the extremities of the front grille opening, the grille being narrowed to accommodate them. On 328 models a new modular side/indicator/driving light unit was provided in the revised front panel, with lens colours again appropriate to the country of sale.

Rear lighting comprised twin circular units on each side of the tail panel through the complete series of cars in the range. On European 308 GTB/S models the outer unit was the orange direction indicator, while the inner unit combined the brake and tail lights with a central reflector; the reversing lights were separate rectangular units set into the bumper immediately below the rear lights. US 308 GTB/S models shared the stop/tail units of European cars, but the reversing lights were incorporated in the centre of the orange direction indicators. With the introduction of the 308 GTBi/Si models, however, all markets received standardised rear light assemblies to the US pattern, with the reversing light in the centre of the indicator unit.

For some markets where legislation decreed, rear fog warning lights were suspended below the bumper on the QV models. For the 328 a pair of high-intensity red rear fog warning lights were fitted in the lower valance panel as standard on European models. US 328s had a slim, rectangular high-level brake light mounted on the inside of the roof, butting up to the top of the rear window. Rear number plate illumination throughout the series was provided by a pair of small rectangular lights in the lower rear edge of the engine lid.

Koni Shock Absorbers

Model	Front	Rear
308 GTB/GTS	82P-1938	82P-1939
308 GTBi/GTSi	82P-1982SP1	82P-1983SP1
308 GTB/GTS QV	82P-1982SP1	82P-1983SP1
328 GTB/GTS	82-2335	82-2336
208 GTB/GTS	82P-1982SP1	82P-1983SP1
208 Turbo	82P-1982SP1	82P-1983SP1
GTB/GTS Turbo	82P-2289	82P-2290

Suspension & Steering

The suspension of all models in the series was identical to that of the 308 GT4 models: independent all round, with unequal-length wishbones, a coil spring and a double-acting Koni shock absorber for each road wheel, plus front and rear anti-roll bars. The construction of the components also followed the description for the 308 GT4 (see pages 28-29).

Where the suspension did differ was in spring rates and shock absorber type and settings, due to the lower weight and different wheelbase of these models. Track and weight differences are given in the table on page 38, while the various Koni shock absorbers and suspension settings for the models in the range are itemised in the panels on this page. All suspension settings, which varied between Berlinetta and Spider versions on the earlier cars, apply to the standard tyre and wheel specifications. If optional wider wheels, or wheels of larger diameter with low-profile tyres, are fitted, these values have to be adjusted in accordance with the manufacturer's recommendations.

In mid-1988 for European 328s and late-1988 for US 328s, the suspension geometry was changed to provide anti-dive and zero offset, concurrently with the preparation to accept the optional – but later standard – ABS braking system.

Steering was by rack and pinion with 3.28 turns lock to lock up to and including the QV or 3.25 turns thereafter, as a result of a slightly higher ratio rack; in

Suspension Settings

Model	Front toe-in	Front camber	Rear toe-in	Rear camber
308 GTB	1-3mm	−0°10′ to −0°30′	3-4mm	−1°05′ to −1°25′
308 GTS	2-3mm	+0°5′ to +0°25′	3.5-4.5mm	−1°05′ to −1°25′
308 GTBi & QV	0.2-1.2mm	−0°10′ to +0°10′	3-4mm	−1°05′ to −1°25′
308 GTSi & QV	0.2-1.2mm	−0°10′ to +0°10′	4-5mm	−1°05′ to −1°25′
328 GTB/S	2-3mm	−0°35′ to −0°55′	3-4mm	−1°50′ to −2°10′
208 GTB	1-3mm	−0°10′ to −0°30′	3-4mm	−1°05′ to −1°25′
208 GTS	2-3mm	+0°5′ to +0°25′	3.5-4.5mm	−1°05′ to −1°25′
208 Turbo	2-3mm	−0°10′ to +0°10′	3-4mm	−1°05′ to −1°25′
GTB/S Turbo	2-3mm	−0°10′ to −0°30′	3-4mm	−1°30′ to −1°50′

Castor angle was fixed, at 4° up to and including the QV models, at 6° on the 328 models, and at 4° 30′ for the GTB/S Turbo. All settings are applicable to a car in static laden condition: full tank of petrol, two persons on board, 20kg of luggage.

Basic five-spoke theme for wheels remained through life of range, but with each new model came subtle revisions. Wheels from carburettor 308 GTB/S (far left) and injection 308 GTBi/Si (left) look similar but there are casting differences. For the 328 (facing page) wheels also differ for models without ABS (concave shape) and with ABS (convex shape).

all instances the turning circle was 12m (39ft). The steering column was collapsible, and steering ball joints were lubrication-free sealed units, with automatic slack take-up facility.

BRAKES

As with many other chassis components, the braking system on all models was virtually identical to that of the 308 GT4, with ventilated discs all round and a tandem master cylinder feeding separate front and rear wheel circuits, incorporating vacuum servo assistance. The brake fluid reservoir was mounted under an access cover, in the shield panel of the front compartment, just forward of the windscreen, with the servo unit alongside. A dashboard warning light advised of pressure loss in either circuit, and also doubled as the handbrake 'on' warning light.

The handbrake was cable-operated, and up to and including the QV models it acted via the rear brake calipers, with a manual slack adjustment assembly at the rear of the car. The 328 and GTB/S Turbo models had conventional brake shoes for the handbrake that acted on the inner surface of the rear disc hubs. To the end of the QV period the brake pads were Ferodo I/D 346GG.

ABS braking became available as an option on the 328 series in mid-1988, and was then standardised from chassis number 76626. The system was a Teves Mark 2, and a failure warning lamp was sited in the bottom left-hand corner of the dash panel. Non-ABS cars up to the introduction of the revised suspension geometry for the optional ABS brakes had flat-spoke wheels, whereas from this point on all cars, whether ABS or not, had convex-spoke wheels.

WHEELS & TYRES

Road wheels were in cast light alloy, always with five-bolt fixing and a five-spoke design, with a small yellow plastic hub centre cap bearing the *Cavallino Rampante* emblem.

However, with each revised model came a change in spoke design, and sometimes also wheel diameter. Together with numerous optional wheels during the life of the range, all this makes for quite a baffling array of specifications that can be considered original equipment. In addition to the varying designs, Ferrari used three manufacturers – Cromodora, Campagnolo and Speedline – to produce wheels, the name usually being found cast in the rim or on the inner face of the wheel hub. Japanese market wheels, which had to pass separate safety standard tests in that country, were stamped 'JWL'.

The table below gives the wheel and tyre combinations as listed in the owner's handbooks.

WHEELS/TYRES

Model	Status	Wheel size	Tyre size
308 GTB/S & 208	Standard	6.5Jx14	Michelin XWX 205/70 R14
	Optional	7.5Jx14	Michelin XWX 205/70 R14
	Spare (EU only)	3.5Jx18	Michelin 105 R 18X
308 GTBi/Si, QV & 208 Turbo[1]	Standard	165 TR 390 FH-PR	Michelin TRX 240/55 VR415
	Optional (not QV)	6.5Jx14	Michelin XWX 205/70 VR14
	Optional (not QV)	7.5Jx14	Michelin XWX 205/70 VR14
	Optional (front)	7Jx16	Pirelli P7 205/55 VR16
	Optional (rear)	8Jx16	Pirelli P7 225/50 VR16
	Spare (EU only)	3.25Bx18	Michelin T105/80 R18
328 GTB/S[2] **& Turbo**	Standard (front)	7Jx16	205/55 VR16[3]
	Standard (rear)	8Jx16	225/50 VR16[3]
	Spare (EU and US)	3.25Bx18	Goodyear T105/80 R18[4]

[1] 208 Turbo is as 308 QV, including options. Although GTBi/Si and QV models had wheels of identical design, the finish was different: the former were plain lacquered silver grey, the latter initially a darker metallic grey with highly polished rims and spoke ridges, before reverting to the previous silver grey finish.
[2] From mid-1988 (EU) and late-1988 (US), with the introduction of revised suspension geometry and optional ABS brakes, wheels were as used on the Mondial t (a convex spoke design, with the centre almost in line with the outer rim); wheel and tyre sizes were unchanged. All cars were fitted with ABS after chassis number 76626.
[3] Specified tyre makes were Goodyear Eagle, Michelin MXW and Pirelli P700; also Goodyear NCT for US only.
[4] Michelin 115/85 R18 was an alternative.

Identification Plates

All cars had identification plates in standard locations. However, during the period in which these models were in production, individual countries introduced their own particular requirements on what identification, advisory and warning labels were required, and in what locations they should be affixed to the vehicle. To list every single variation, its message and location, would fill a book in itself. This section therefore establishes the main identifying marks and their locations, with reference to specific market details, to give an idea of the type of information provided.

1 All models had a plate fixed to the engine block in the centre of the vee, at the cam belt drive end, indicating the engine type and individual serial numbers.
2 An aluminium identification plate was fixed horizontally on a flat panel, between the right-hand top chassis tube and edge of the engine compartment, giving homologation details, engine and chassis type numbers, plus individual chassis number.
3 The chassis number, model type and – from GTBi/Si models onwards – the Vehicle Identification Number (VIN) were stamped in the chassis tube adjacent to this plate. See page 126 for guidance about how to decode the useful VIN information.
4 On European GTB/S models a European Specifications Conformity Plate was in a similar location on the left-hand side of the compartment; US versions had an air pollution plate in this location.
5 On the upper face of the steering column was an aluminium plate set in an upstand, giving model type and individual chassis number, which from the GTBi/Si onwards included the VIN.

To indicate the plethora of labels to be found, a US model 308 GTBi will serve as an example. In the engine compartment there was the engine label in the centre of the vee, the vehicle identification and chassis number on the right-hand top chassis tube, an air pollution plate (different on Californian cars) on the left of the compartment, labels on the primary air box for firing order and engine/gearbox lubricants, a label on the cooling system header tank for anti-freeze solution, and finally a paint specification label affixed to the underside of the lid. Inside the car labels were just as prolific, with the identification plate on top of the steering column, a conformity standards label and catalyst label on the driver's door post, an FMV safety label on the driver's door post, an FMV safety label referring to tyre data and car capacity on the inside of the glovebox lid (on the driver's sun visor on the GTS); Californian cars had a further windscreen sticker for conformity to that state's standards. An 'unleaded fuel only' label was affixed to the inside of the fuel filler flap.

Even the spacesaver spare wheel received its fair share of labelling, with all markets getting an instruction label affixed to it, but the Italian, Dutch and Swedish cars had to have a different instruction label mounted on the rim instead of a spoke, and for these markets, plus Switzerland and Austria, a spare wheel homologation plate had to be provided in the wheel well.

On European market models up to and including the QV, the recommended tyre pressures were indicated on a sticker in the lower corner of the windscreen on the driver's side. On 328 and GTB/S Turbo cars the label was affixed to the inside of the glovebox lid.

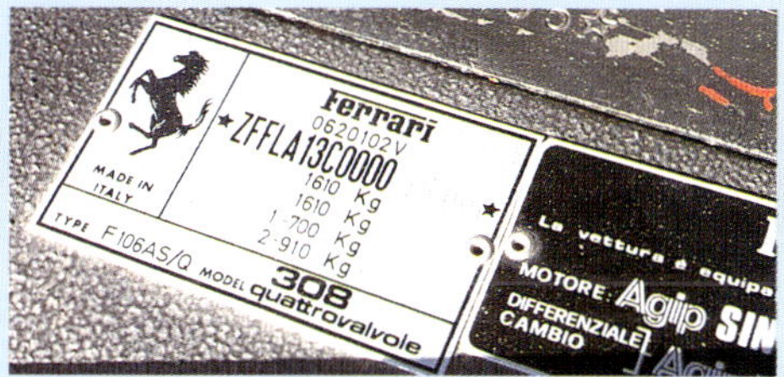

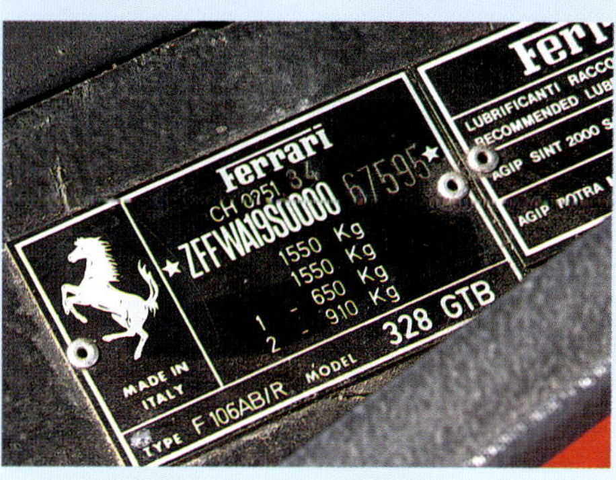

Examples of engine bay identification plates on 308 GTB, 308 QV and 328 GTB. Adjacent stamped-in numbering is seen on earlier pair of models: on 308 GTB this repeats chassis number and model type data found on plate, but on QV it gives Vehicle Identification Number (VIN).

Production Data

Model	Production period	Chassis number range	Number built
308 GTB (glass-fibre)	1975-77	18677-21289	712
308 GTB (steel)	1977-80	20805-34349	2185
308 GTS	1977-80	22619-34501	3219
208 GTB	1980-82	31219-41329	160
208 GTS	1980-82	31249-41265	140
308 GTBi	1980-82	31327-43059	494
308 GTSi	1980-82	31309-43079	1749
208 GTB Turbo	1982-85	41357-59277	437
308 GTB QV	1982-85	42809-59071	748
308 GTS QV	1982-85	41701-59265	3042
208 GTS Turbo	1983-85	42863-59279	250
328 GTB	1985-89	58735-83017	1344
328 GTS	1985-89	59301-83136	6068
GTB Turbo	1986-89	63277-83137	308
GTS Turbo	1986-89	63739-83148	828

MONDIAL SERIES (1980-93)

Mondial 8 in profile shows forward cabin arrangement to maximise interior space – windscreen base comes almost to front wheel centre line. Large, deep glass area provides good all-round visibility, while trapezoidal rear wing air intake and heavy black plastic bumpers are also evident.

The Pininfarina-designed Mondial 8 was presented at the 1980 Geneva Salon, as the replacement for the Bertone-designed 308 GT4. The title Mondial was a resurrection of the name used for one of Ferrari's successful sports racing models of the mid-1950s. The initial impression was that the Mondial 8 appeared much bulkier than its predecessor. Comparing the relative dimensions of the two models confirmed this to be the case, with increases of 100mm (3.9in) in wheelbase, 280mm (11.0in) in overall length, 80mm (3.1in) in width and 40mm (1.6in) in height.

The Mondial 8 was the first V8 model to receive the fuel-injected engine that resulted in a lower power output on the 308 GTBi/Si models. In combination with the bigger, heavier and less aerodynamic body of the Mondial 8, therefore, the performance left a little to be desired by Ferrari standards.

The difficulty of providing 2+2 accommodation with a mid-engined configuration, even allowing for the general increase in dimensions over the 308 GT4, still posed the problem of providing an aesthetically balanced body shape. Pininfarina's offering on the Mondial 8 was conservative, but provided an airy cabin with a large glass area which offered good all-round visibility. The large black plastic bumper mouldings made the front and rear look heavy, and the large trapezoidal body side intake grilles spoiled the profile, especially on early production cars when they were painted matt black. When subsequently painted body colour they looked slightly better, but still could be regarded as incongruous.

The uninspiring appearance and lack-lustre performance did little to promote healthy sales, but in 1982, along with its two-seater V8 sisters, the model gained four-valve cylinder heads and became the Mondial Quattrovalvole. As with the 308 models, this provided a useful boost in performance that helped

There is virtually nothing externally to differentiate Mondial QV from Mondial 8 apart from tail panel badge on coupés, although Mondial 8 was never available as a cabriolet. Side marker lights on front and rear wings identify this car as a US version.

sales figures. At the same time changes were made to the interior trim and instrument layout.

In September 1983 a cabriolet version joined the range, presented to the press by Enzo Ferrari in a ceremony at the Military Academy in Modena during an international Ferrari meeting. The soft-top was designed to replicate the roof profile of the coupé version when raised, even down to the buttresses of the rear pillars. However, the necessity for soft-top stowage space reduced rear seat accommodation. The soft-top itself was retained by two handles on the windscreen rail, manually operated, with a stowage cover in the closed position. The main market target for the cabriolet was the west coast of the US, where full open-top motoring was very popular. This was the first full cabriolet (or Spider) in the Ferrari catalogue for a decade, since the 365 GTB/4 Daytona Spider ceased production in 1973.

The next evolution in the Mondial range occurred in 1985, with the announcement of the Mondial 3.2 at the Frankfurt Salon, concurrently with the 328 range. The increased engine capacity provided similar benefits to those of the two-seater models. The Mondial also received revised front and rear lower body panel designs, which improved its appearance, and a closer family resemblance was achieved by adopting body colour bumpers and a similar grille design to the 328. The road wheel design also changed, together with alterations to the interior trim and instruments.

The final change to the Mondial, which never really lived up to sales expectations, came in 1989 with the announcement of the Mondial t, the t denoting transverse gearbox. The engine increased in size to 3405cc, and its alignment became longitudinal instead of transverse. Visually this model can be recognised by the much neater, and more discreet, rectangular air intakes on reprofiled rear wings. The interior

Rear three-quarter views of cabriolet with soft-top erected and stowed provide an appearance comparison, and also show how soft-top lines follow general shape of coupé buttress treatment. Also evident on this US model is exhaust silencer shield and increased rear bumper projection.

once again was revamped to coincide with the model change. Late in the production run an electronically operated clutch designed by Valeo became available as an option. This permitted normal gear changing, with clutch actuation via sophisticated electronics.

The Mondial t continued in production until 1993, when, without any formal announcement, it faded out of production, although new examples could still be found in dealers' showrooms in 1995. Throughout the period of production, the only visual differences on US versions were rectangular side marker lights on the front and rear wings, an exhaust silencer protection shield on Mondial 8 and QV models, and minor light lens variations.

BODY & CHASSIS

Chassis construction followed conventional Ferrari practice of main large-section oval steel tubes for the central structure. These extended forward to pick up the front suspension frame, and rearward with a 'Y' branch each side where large, rectangular, bolted flanges picked up the engine and rear suspension frame. The purpose of these flanges was to permit unitary removal of the engine/transmission/suspension assembly from beneath the car, rather than having to lift it through the engine cover, thus easing maintenance procedures.

Supplementary frames for suspension, steering, engine, door posts and body mounting were constructed from rectangular and square-section steel

DIMENSIONS & WEIGHTS

Mondial 8	**Europe**	**US**
Overall length	4580mm (180.3in)	4640mm (182.7in)
Overall width	1790mm (70.5in)	1790mm (70.5in)
Overall height	1250mm (49.2in)	1250mm (49.2in)
Wheelbase	2650mm (104.3in)	2650mm (104.3in)
Front track	1495mm (58.9in)	1513mm (58.9in)
Rear track	1517mm (59.7in)	1535mm (59.7in)
Luggage compartment	300 litres	250 litres
Dry weight	1504kg (3315lb)	1586kg (3496lb)
Mondial QV	**Europe**	**US**
Overall height, coupé	1260mm (49.6in)	1260mm (49.6in)
Overall height, cabrio	1290mm (50.8in)	1290mm (50.8in)
Dry weight, coupé	1490kg (3284lb)	1551kg (3419lb)
Dry weight, cabrio	1430kg (3152lb)	1491kg (3286lb)
Mondial 3.2	**Europe**	**US**
Overall length	4535mm (178.5in)	4535mm (178.5in)
Overall width	1795mm (70.7in)	1795mm (70.7in)
Overall height, coupé	1235mm (48.6in)	1235mm (48.6in)
Overall height, cabrio	1265mm (49.8in)	1265mm (49.8in)
Wheelbase	2650mm (104.3in)	2650mm (104.3in)
Front track	1520mm (59.8in)	1520mm (59.8in)
Rear track	1510mm (59.4in)	1510mm (59.4in)
Dry weight, coupé	1410kg (3108lb)	1540kg (3395lb)
Dry weight, cabrio	1400kg (3086lb)	1530kg (3373lb)
Mondial t	**Europe**	**US**
Overall width	1810mm (71.3in)	1810mm (71.3in)
Front track	1522mm (59.9in)	1522mm (59.9in)
Rear track	1560mm (61.4in)	1560mm (61.4in)
Dry weight, coupé	1503kg (3313lb)	1560kg (3439lb)
Dry weight, cabrio	1536kg (3386lb)	1570kg (3461lb)

Note For models after Mondial 8, measurements are given only where they changed.

OPTIONAL EQUIPMENT

Metallic paint
Electric sunroof (coupé)
Leather soft-top cover (cabrio)
ABS braking (early 3.2 Mondials, thereafter standard)
Leather dashboard (3.2 coupé & t coupé/cabrio)
Leather headlining and rear window surround (3.2 & t coupé)
Spare wheel (optional only on Mondial t)
Leather luggage, by Schedoni

Cabriolet soft-top arrangement in detail: taut in raised position, midway through folding operation, and stowed under its fitted cover in lowered position.

tube. Additional bracing was provided for bumper mounting, and between the passenger and engine compartment on US market models to meet tougher crash test requirements. The floor pan, inner wheel arches and front bulkhead were constructed from steel, welded to the chassis. As with other Ferrari models, there was an insulated sandwich firewall between the cabin and engine bay, with insulated steel sandwich linings to the rear luggage compartment. Similarly an undertray was fitted below the passenger compartment, as on the other V8 models. Cabriolets had additional strengthening gussets on the door hinge and shut posts, and also a deeper sill section to increase body rigidity, due to the lack of a roof.

The main body panels were steel pressings, the

Mondial 3.2's new front grille and light arrangement – shared with contemporary 328 GTB/S – smoothed lines considerably, and convex-pattern wheels were fitted. Rear view shows new colour-coded bumper/valance, more aesthetically pleasing than heavy black plastic bumpers of earlier models, and new full-width grille covering silencer. This car has non-standard colour-coded door mirrors.

High-level shot of Mondial 3.2 provides possibly one of its most attractive views, and shows optional electrically operated sunroof available on coupé.

Mondial t, here in cabriolet form, was final evolution. Identifying features are neater rectangular rear wing air intake grilles and more bulbous profile of rear wings themselves.

only exceptions being the aluminium front lid and rear engine cover used on the Mondial 8 and QV. On the 3.2 and t models the lower front and rear body panel/bumper units were manufactured in glass-fibre. The bumpers on the Mondial 8 and QV were three-piece black plastic mouldings.

The cabriolets had a manually operated, heavy-duty canvas soft-top with a Plexiglas rear screen. The top was retained by two locking handles on the front windscreen rail, and provided with a matching cover retained by stud fasteners when in the folded position. Because the soft-top reduced the size of the engine cover, and thus access to the forward bank of cylinders, a removable cover was provided in the rear bulkhead to facilitate routine servicing on the QV and 3.2 cabriolets; this was unnecessary on the Mondial t because of its longitudinal engine placement.

A towing eye was provided in the right-hand side of the grille opening on the Mondial 8, while QV models had an eye that screwed into a socket in a similar location and doubled as the spare wheel retaining bolt. The 3.2 and t models also had a removable towing eye that screwed into sockets in the right-hand side of the grille opening, but these formed part of the tool kit.

BODY TRIM & FITTINGS

Mondial bodies were virtually devoid of any bright trim throughout the production period. All had polished aluminium egg-crate grilles to the front radiator air intake, those on the 3.2 and t models featuring a polished aluminium *Cavallino Rampante*.

The Mondial 8, QV and 3.2 models had slim, oval, chromed door handles, but the t versions were body coloured and of a different design. All models carried slim, rectangular, aluminium 'Disegno di Pininfarina' badges on both lower body sides between the door and rear wheel arch. A chrome *Cavallino Rampante* was fixed to the left-hand side of the tail panel between the number plate location and tail lights. To match this, the model designation badge was provided on the right: on the Mondial 8 this was rectangular and made of aluminium, but the badge on subsequent models was black anodised aluminium with white inset script. An aluminium 'Ferrari' script badge was fixed to the upper rear edge of the rear luggage compartment lid, and an enamel Ferrari shield was fitted in the centre of the leading edge of the front lid.

The screens had black rubber surrounds, while the door and side window frames had a matt black finish.

Mondial t coupé in black, which helps to disguise black plastic sections on rear buttresses, window surrounds and door mirrors, making overall shape more homogeneous. Effect of dark colours on Mondial 8 and QV models, with their black plastic bumpers, is even more noticeable.

US cabriolet version of Mondial t, also in black, shows how two sides of Atlantic had closed gap on legislation. Only really noticeable difference is side marker lights, although careful look reveals that top edge of grille opening is stepped down inboard of light on each side, to accommodate impact absorbers. Shape of rear wing engine intake (right) changed from trapezoidal to rectangular for Mondial t.

Tinted glass was standard on all models, with a heavily tinted band across the windscreen top, and all coupés were provided with a heated rear screen. Windscreen wipers parked on the right on left-hand drive cars and on the left on right-hand drive models. A single electrically adjustable mirror with a black plastic casing was fitted to the driver's door on the Mondial 8, but QV, 3.2 and t versions were fitted with a pair of mirrors with matt black casings virtually identical to those of the earlier models, again with remote electric operation.

The front and rear bumper assemblies on the Mondial 8 and QV were three-piece wrap-round units in grained black plastic. There was a barely perceptible additional projection on US market cars. Bumpers on 3.2 and t versions were incorporated into the front and rear lower body panels and finished in body colour. The US 3.2 and t versions had two rectangular projections from the top edge into the grille openings to accommodate the impact absorber supports. European Mondial 8 and QV models had a plain body-colour valance below the rear bumper

External door release catch and lock assembly also changed for Mondial t, earlier bright, teardrop-shaped design having also been used on 400 series Ferraris.

Tail badging through range: Mondial 8, Mondial QV, Mondial cabriolet, Mondial 3.2 and Mondial t.

Mondial 8 interior (facing page, top) shows style of deep-pleated seat stitching that remained through to 3.2. Note heating/ventilation controls on underslung panel below dashboard. Wooden gearknob is after-market accessory to replace correct black plastic ball, a design shared with later models. Mondial QV interior (facing page, bottom) is unchanged in general design, but note revised centre console containing heating/ventilation controls, electric mirror control on door, steering wheel with solid spokes and 'quattrovalvole' motif on glovebox.

incorporating rear fog lights, but on US versions the centre section was a deeper matt black louvred cover over the exhaust silencer, while louvres outboard of the exhaust tail-pipes also replaced the fog warning lights found on European models.

All Mondials had separate rear lids for the engine and luggage compartment. The engine cover lid on coupés was largely plain with a row of only seven full-width louvres towards the rear edge, but cabriolets had louvres over the whole surface area of a smaller lid. The front luggage compartment lid of all models had a row of five full-width louvres behind the retractable headlight pods, in order to allow hot air to escape from the radiator.

On Mondial 8, QV, and 3.2 models, large trapezoidal grilles were provided in the upper body sides, between the doors and rear wheel arches, to cover engine air inlets. On the Mondial t these became smaller, more elegant rectangular grilles, on more bulbous reprofiled rear wings.

The fuel filler was located behind a hinged panel on the left-hand rear roof pillar on coupés or on the left-hand rear wing on cabriolets. This fed twin fuel tanks located under the rear seat area on Mondial 8, QV and 3.2 models, or a single tank in the same location on the t version. The lids for the engine bay and front and rear luggage compartments were released by solenoids actuated by interior switches, with manual pull rings provided for emergency use in the event of an electrical failure.

An electrically operated sunroof was available as an option on coupés throughout the production period.

PAINTWORK

As with the 308 series from 1980 and subsequent 328 and 348 series which paralleled Mondial production, paint was supplied by Glasurit and the range of colours available was identical, as detailed in the charts on pages 43 and 89. The sill panels were finished in matt black underseal throughout production.

INTERIOR TRIM & FITTINGS

Due to the increase in wheelbase and width over the 308 GT4, the interior of the Mondial provided a far more acceptable 2+2 seating arrangement – in fact with a short driver the car could almost be considered a full four-seater.

All passengers were provided with individual bucket seats with head restraints front and rear on coupés, but for the front only on cabriolets. The seats were trimmed in leather, as were the door and rear side panels. The front seats were adjustable for fore/aft movement and rake, with facility to recline. Fore/aft movement was controlled by a bar under the front of the seat squab on all models. On Mondials up to and including the 3.2 rake was adjusted by a knurled knob on the inner lower edge of the backrest, while a separate lever on the outer lower edge of the backrest angled it forward to allow access to the rear seats; on the Mondial t a single dual-purpose lever controlled these functions.

The rear seats were fixed on all coupés up to and

Mondial 3.2 interior (left) shows one of the more striking leather/carpet colour combinations available, but changes are confined to small details such as door catch position and angled top corners on instrument panel surround. Mondial t interior (below) was comprehensively updated. Besides revised door trims, new instrument panel and upswept centre console (all highlighted in later pictures), seats, steering wheel and passenger side of dashboard have changed. This car has non-standard but attractive over-carpets.

Rear compartment comparison between coupé (Mondial 8) and cabriolet (QV) shows that seats were set much closer together on open car, to allow soft-top stowage room either side; cabriolet rear seats also lack head restraints.

Mondial t coupé rear compartment (below) differs in many details – design of seats, console and armrest – but also for the facility for one or both seat backrests, less head restraints on coupés, to fold forward to create a luggage platform. Mondial t cabriolet (below right) has also moved on, with a little more space between seats but an intrusive arrangement for central inertia reel mountings for front seat belts.

Mondial 3.2 rear compartment differs only in detail from earlier cars – note shape of armrest and presence of storage locker above – but this view shows useful increase in legroom compared with shorter-wheelbase 308 GT4; centre console extends back to house ventilation flaps, ashtray and cigarette lighter.

Door panels from Mondial 8 (this page, left), QV cabrio (right), 3.2 (facing page, left) and t (right): overall design remained similar through model run, but there were detail changes to oddment pocket design, door pull arrangement and switch positions.

including the 3.2. The Mondial t coupé featured folding seat backrests released by a pull catch adjacent to the outer edges of the head restraints, which were separate and fixed to the rear bulkhead. The rear faces of the backrests were carpeted and provided a luggage platform when lowered, and each backrest had a pair of leather luggage-restraining straps. This feature was found on all cabriolets, prompted by the necessity for a removable panel in the rear bulkhead for access to the engine for maintenance.

Stitching and upholstery padding styles of the seats remained unchanged until the Mondial t was introduced. Deeper side bolsters to squab and backrest were provided on this model, and the stitch pattern of the centre panel changed. Throughout the coupé range each seat, front and rear, was fitted with lap and diagonal inertia reel seat belts, but cabriolets differed in having only lap belts in the rear.

The roof lining and rear pillars were lined with a fine beige/brown or black/grey stripe material throughout the series, although from 1987 the Mondial 3.2 coupé could be provided, as an option at an extra cost, with a leather dashboard and/or leather headlining plus rear window surround. This option continued for the Mondial t coupé, with the addition of an optional leather dashboard and/or soft-top stowage cover for the cabriolet version.

The floor, inner sills, wheel arches and a triangular section on the front corner of the door panels were carpeted in a colour compatible with the interior trim, from a range of five colours. Upholstery and carpet colours were shared with contemporary 308/328/348 models, as detailed on pages 43/44 and 89. The driver's mat featured a black rubber heel pad. The front section of the centre tunnel was also carpeted on all models except the Mondial t, which had a console over this area.

The basic interior door and side panel design changed very little during production, with only the position and type of handles and switches affecting the overall appearance, all cabriolets, 3.2 models from chassis number 64633(LHD), 64183(RHD), 64531(USA), and Mondial t models featured an open door pull, instead of the finger-slot type provided on the earlier models. The radio speakers were concealed behind perforations in the door panel leather on all models except the Mondial QV coupe, where they were surface mounted.

All models featured electric windows as standard, removable plugs being provided – in keeping with standard Ferrari practice – in the door panels to insert a crank handle in the event of motor failure. Cabriolets also had electrically operated side glasses to the rear compartment. Twin sun visors were provided, the passenger's one containing a vanity mirror. Interior illumination was by central roof-mounted lights front and rear in the coupés, but in the front only – between the sun visors – in the cabriolets. The dipping interior mirror was attached to the windscreen by an adhesive pad.

Air conditioning was another standard feature on all Mondials. It fed through the heating and ventilation system, the pump being mounted in the engine compartment and belt-driven off the engine. Up to and including the 3.2 a stereo radio/cassette player with speakers and electrical aerial was supplied as standard equipment. With the introduction of the Mondial t, the speakers and aerial were still provided but no stereo equipment, Ferrari's view being that many clients preferred to choose their own from an ever more sophisticated array available.

The steering wheel was always leather-covered with three spokes, those on the Mondial 8 being matt black, each with a central longitudinal slot. QV and 3.2 models had plain matt black spokes, while the t had a completely redesigned wheel with a triangulated centre section around the *Cavallino Rampante* badge, thumb rests set into the two horizontal spokes, and a Momo logo in the vertical spoke.

The main instruments were displayed in a long, horizontal, rectangular binnacle that projected from the dash panel. The binnacle and top dash panel had a black vinyl covering, a theme that extended along the door tops and rear compartment to the engine bulkhead. The lower dash panel was upholstered to match the interior colour. This arrangement was constant throughout the range of models. On models up to and including the 3.2 the front face of the passenger side of the dash featured a glovebox inside which was an adjustable map-reading light with its own switch, while the Mondial t had a glovebox in the top face with an interior light and a socket for a portable lamp. Additional storage was provided by pockets in the doors.

On all models the handbrake was on the outside of the driver's seat.

DASHBOARD & INSTRUMENTS

Inside the Mondial, it was the instrument panel and the centre control console that underwent the most changes during the life of the model. The Mondial was the most 'electronic' model produced by Ferrari at the time of its introduction, and the instrumentation, featuring a modular bank of warning lights and a check panel among other deviations from standard practice, was more futuristic than had previously been seen on a car from the Maranello stable.

The basic overall shape of the dash and centre console did not alter during the production period, but the location of the contents did with almost every model change. The layouts are described in turn.

The instrument panel on the Mondial 8 contained white-on-black dials. Starting on the left, there was a bank of six square push-button switches in three rows of two, comprising – in a clockwise direction from bottom left – rear fog lights, front fog lights, heated rear window, front lid release, engine lid release and rear boot release. Next came the rev counter (with a yellow zone from 7000rpm and a red zone from 7800rpm), a vertical bank of 12 warning lights, the speedometer, and a panel containing at the top a digital electronic clock and below it the distance recorder above the trip meter. Alongside this panel was another slim one containing, from top to bottom, clock control switches, instrument panel light rheostat and trip meter setting knob. The display was completed by a panel containing a bank of four dials covering, anti-clockwise from bottom left, oil pressure, fuel, water temperature and oil temperature.

There were two stalks to the left of the steering column, the larger one controlling lights and the shorter one direction indicators. One stalk to the right of the column controlled windscreen wipers and washers. In the centre of the dash between the steering column and glovebox was a pair of rectangular ventilation air outlets. On a sub-panel on the lower centre edge of the dashboard were the ventilation, heating and air conditioning controls.

The centre console had the open gate and gear lever in the front corner on the driver's side, with an ashtray alongside it containing a cigarette lighter. To the rear of these was a bank of five switches and the external mirror adjustment lever: the switches controlled electric windows left and right, parking lights, fuel filler cover and electric aerial. The panel then dropped to a lower level, with a radio/cassette unit fitted in the vertical face. On the lower horizontal face was a systems monitor panel containing a bank of warning lights for 10 specific functions, plus a yellow warning light for any failure in items 6-10, a red one for items 1-5 and a green one for no failures displayed. The tunnel was completed by the front seat belt catches, either side of the rear ashtray.

The main dashboard panel and steering column controls remained virtually unchanged for the QV,

Four instrument panel variations over Mondial life span: long rectangle for 8 (top left) and QV (top right), rectangle with angled top corners for 3.2 (above left), and deep, heavily shrouded nacelle for t (above right).

although the rev counter and speedometer changed places. The supplementary lower dash ventilation control panel was omitted, the controls being integrated into a completely revised centre console which now extended forwards and upwards to house the radio/cassette player ahead of the gear lever. The door mirror control switches moved from the centre console to the driver's door panel.

The gearchange gate and lever maintained the same location but alongside it now was the systems monitor panel, with a push-button hazard warning light switch behind it. To the rear of these was a full-width ashtray and then a longitudinal bank of four push-button switches for the air conditioning controls. Alongside these was a bank of six rocker switches for glovebox lid, parking lights, fuel filler cover, electric windows left and right, and electric radio aerial. This section of the panel was completed by two air conditioning rotary switches and a cigarette lighter. The seat belt catches now had a covered cassette holder between them, while two circular ventilation outlets, an ashtray and a cigarette lighter were provided for rear seat occupants.

The Mondial's evolution to 3.2 form for once meant little change to the instrumentation or switch layout. The instrument faces now featured orange markings on a black background, the central bank of warning lights on the dashboard was modified slightly, and the column control stalks were redesigned but still performed the same functions.

With the introduction of the t model, the main dashboard received its most significant revision of the whole period, losing numerous switches that were relocated on a further modified forward section of the centre console. The dashboard thus became narrower and slightly taller.

In the bottom left-hand corner was the fuel gauge, with the water temperature warning light above it. Next came the speedometer, now incorporating distance/trip meters and warning lights for direction indicators, main beam and 'lights on'. In the centre was the oil pressure gauge with the water temperature gauge above it, and to the right of these the rev counter containing warning lights for handbrake/front pad wear, ABS failure and alternator. In the bottom right-hand corner was the engine oil temperature gauge with above it (on the cabriolet only) a rear electric side window mechanism lock warning light.

Parallel changes to Mondial centre console layout for same four models: 8 (top left), QV (top right), 3.2 (above left) and t (above right). Gearchange was always on driver's side of console.

These instruments were surmounted by a horizontal bank of 12 different function warning lights.

The electric window switches moved from the centre console to the door pull cut-outs that were introduced with this model. The new sloped, vertical section of the dash featured a digital clock at top centre, with switches for shock absorber settings (left) and hazard warning lights (right) on either side. Below these was a bank of five switches to release the glovebox lid, fuel filler flap, front lid, engine cover and rear boot. Under these was a compartment for the stereo unit. Apart from the relocation of the electric window and hazard warning switches the remainder of the centre console layout was virtually unchanged. Dials remained orange-on-black, as on the 3.2 model.

On all cabriolet models, the electric side rear window control switches were provided at the back of the centre console, between the cassette holder and rear ventilation outlets.

Since the Mondial had been designed as a 'world market' car, far fewer alterations were necessary to the instrumentation to meet various market regulations, specific warning light requirements being incorporated into the panels supplied.

LUGGAGE COMPARTMENT

The main luggage compartment was under its own lid at the rear of the car, behind the engine compartment. As was the case with other Ferraris with the boot in this location, care had to be taken as to what was stowed in it, due to the heat build-up. The compartment was fully carpeted and the lid was supported by a gas-filled strut.

As with the two-seater models, stowage space in the front compartment was limited to small, soft baggage around the spare wheel, except in the Mondial t, for which a spare wheel was an option. Obviously this released additional space for luggage in the front compartment wheel well.

The front-mounted radiator and fans were separated from the main area by a shield that formed the spare wheel carrier. The battery was sited in the right-hand corner of this front section and provided with a rotating kill switch adjacent to it. In the left-hand corner was the air conditioning condenser coil. Twin trumpet air horns were common to the range, mounted behind the right-hand front cover of the radiator grille.

Rear luggage compartment of Mondial 8 (far left) remained virtually unchanged throughout series, while front compartment of Mondial t (above, with optional spare wheel) was much the same as it had been at the start.

In the main compartment under the front lid, the screen washer bottle was mounted in the right-hand side of the dividing shield, with the fuse/relay board on the left. On the left-hand side of the bulkhead could be found the brake master cylinder, reservoir and servo unit. On the 3.2 and t models a hydraulic clutch was used, with the master cylinder behind the pedal, using a common reservoir with the brakes. On 3.2 and t models where an ABS braking system was employed, the electronic control unit was on the right-hand side of the compartment.

Fitted luggage sets, manufactured in leather by Schedoni of Modena, maximised luggage-carrying capacity and were available as an optional extra throughout the range.

The tool kit on Mondial 8 models came in two separate soft vinyl bags, one mounted on the spare wheel and the other under a panel on the left of the rear boot. On Mondial QV and 3.2 models the kit was again in two soft vinyl bags, but now both were mounted on the spare wheel. On the Mondial t the tool kit was contained in a rigid leather case mounted in the spare wheel well. The contents of the tool kit were virtually identical to those of concurrent two-seater models, the only differences being the provision of a battery removal handle, a plug-in emergency light and an emergency handle for manual operation of the sunroof on the Mondial 8, QV and 3.2 coupés.

ENGINE

The engines fitted in the Mondials were of identical specification to those in their two-seater counterparts, although they were given their own range of identification numbers. No Italian market 2-litre version was ever produced, the reasoning probably being that the performance of the Mondial 8 was regarded as sluggish by Ferrari standards, so a 2-litre version would have been totally unviable. The Mondial was the first road Ferrari to receive a fuel-injected engine from the start of its production run.

The Mondial 8 engine was equivalent to that in the 308 GTBi/Si, and likewise the Quattrovalvole to the 308 QV models, the 3.2 Mondial to the 328 series and the Mondial t to the 348 series.

On all models the exhaust silencer was mounted transversely across the tail below the boot, and the catalytic converter, where fitted, was sited behind it. On the Mondial t there were twin transverse silencers, with a separate catalytic converter for each bank of cylinders installed as supplementary silencers, without a catalytic 'monolith'. As with early European 348 models, the first examples were not fitted with catalytic converters but could run on either leaded or unleaded fuel. Exhaust gases exited through twin pairs of chromed pipes, in rear valance cut-outs on the Mondial 8 and QVs, and through an opening in the louvred valance panel on the 3.2 and t models.

SYSTEM CAPACITIES (LITRES)

Model	Fuel	Cooling	Washer	Engine oil	Gearbox oil
Mondial	84	15	2	9	4
Mondial QV	87	15	2	10	4
Mondial 3.2	80	24	2	10	4
Mondial t	96/86[1]	20	3	11	4

[1] Cabriolet fuel tank capacity.

Transverse engine layout on pre-1989 Mondials, seen here in a QV (facing page, top), was very similar to that of parallel 308/328 models, but cooling system header tank at bottom left was a different shape to suit shorter compartment. As on two-seaters, injection intake castings became progressively more elegant through Mondial 8, QV and 3.2 periods. Biggest change of all for Mondial t (facing page, bottom): V8 is aligned longitudinally, necessitating different intake arrangements and new positions for some ancillaries, such as cooling system header tank. Notice all that extra room around engine…

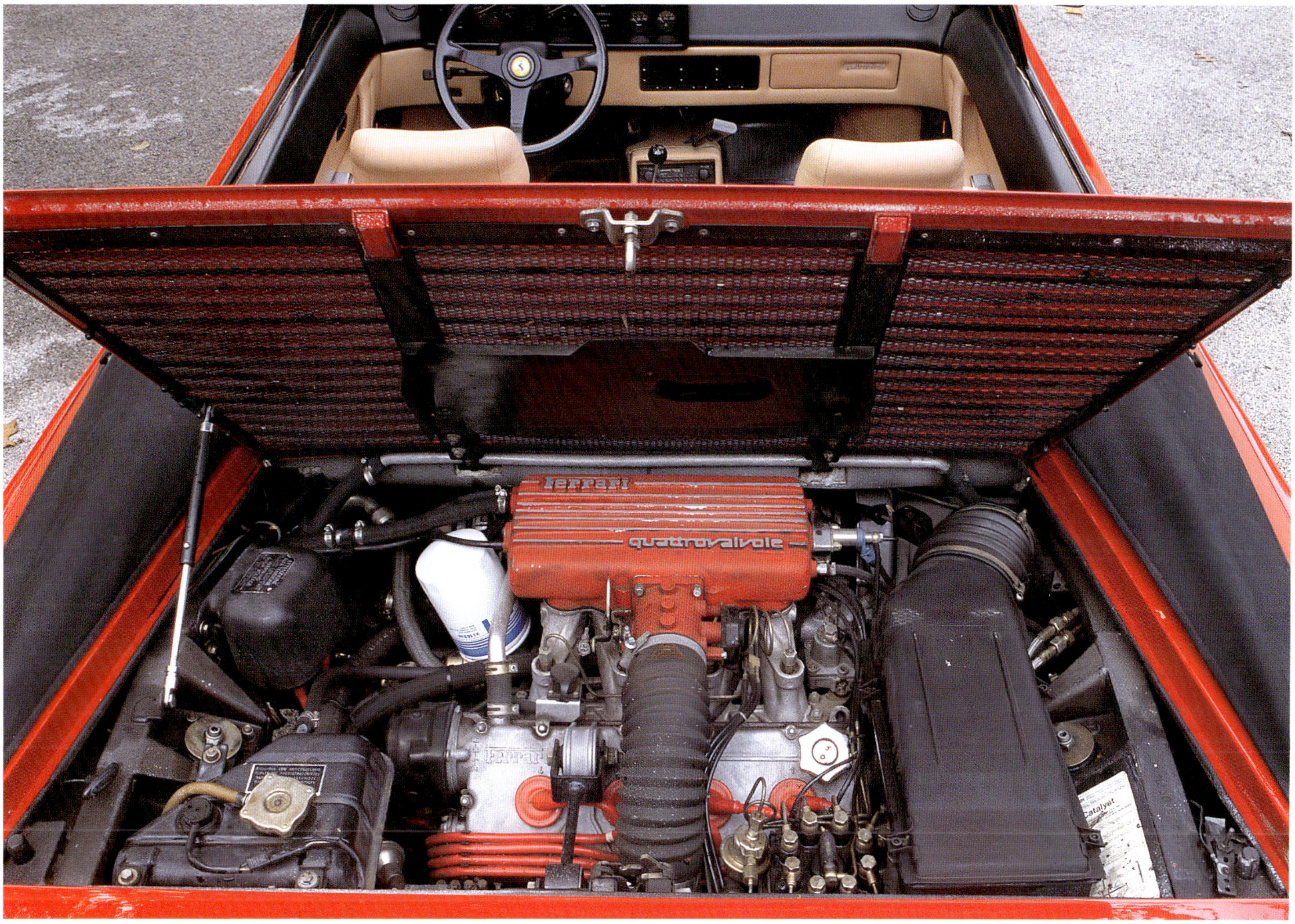
Ferrari
quattrovalvole

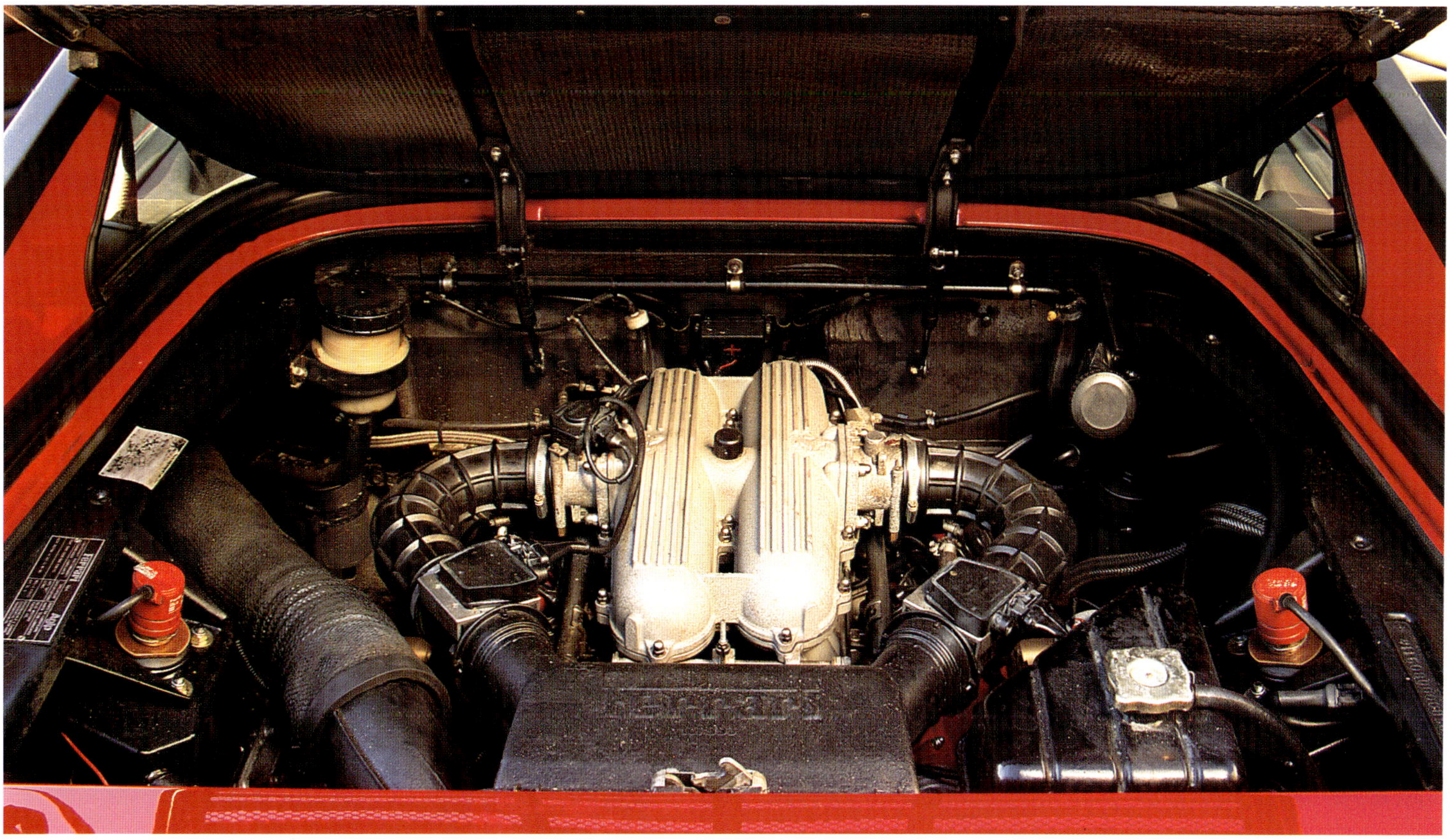

OVERALL GEAR RATIOS

Mondial 8 & QV	All markets[1]
First	1:13.888
Second	1:9.559
Third	1:6.878
Fourth	1:5.055
Fifth	1:3.736
Reverse	1:13.194
Final drive	16/65

Mondial 3.2	All markets
First	1:13.072
Second	1:8.996
Third	1:6.473
Fourth	1:4.756
Fifth	1:3.514
Reverse	1:12.419
Final drive	17/65

Mondial t	All markets
First	1:12.517
Second	1:8.198
Third	1:5.676
Fourth	1:4.260
Fifth	1:3.354
Reverse	1:10.847
Final drive	16/57

[1] Switzerland was an exception, Mondial QVs for this market having the same ratios as the Swiss-specification 308 QV.

Optional Valeo automatic clutch on Mondial t gave two-pedal control while retaining a conventional gearchange.

TRANSMISSION

Again the transmission assembly followed the layout and structure of the equivalent two-seater models, but all models apart from the Mondial 8, which shared gear and final drive ratios with the 308 GTBi/Si, had their own ratios, as listed in the panel above.

The clutch operation on the Mondial series differed from the two-seater models in that it was hydraulically actuated via a master cylinder directly in front of the pedal box. The clutch fluid reservoir was separate on Mondial 8 and QV models, but a combined clutch/brake fluid reservoir was found on 3.2 and t models.

Late in the production period of the Mondial t, a fully automatic clutch, developed by the French company Valeo, was introduced as an option. This innovative development gave two-pedal operation without sacrificing a normal gearchange. The heart of the system was a sophisticated electronic control unit that received information from sensors on the ignition switch, gear lever, throttle, gearbox input shaft and gearshift position mechanism. The 'brain' then read the information obtained and transmitted a message to an electro-mechanical clutch actuator (mounted on the bellhousing), which engaged or disengaged the clutch in less than 100 milliseconds. The system incorporated numerous safety features, preventing the car being started if in gear, or preventing selection of too low a gear on downshifts relative to road speed, with a warning buzzer to indicate the problem. This also sounded if a gear was engaged with the door open, or if the driver tried to pull away in too high a gear.

ELECTRICAL EQUIPMENT & LIGHTS

The electrical system for all models was 12-volt negative earth, served from a 66Ah battery fed by an alternator. Specifications for the main electrical components are given in the panel.

Lighting on the Mondials was designed for world markets from the outset, and thus, apart from US/Japan side marker light requirements, there was little visible difference between the different market models, although exact specifications varied – lens colours, bulb wattage and dipping arrangements. All lights were manufactured by Carello.

The headlights on the Mondial 8, QV and 3.2 models were twin 5in diameter units mounted in pods, the outer light for dipped beam and the inner one for main beam. The Mondial t had a slim, rectangular, homofocal unit in each pod, the outer section being dipped beam and the inner main beam. The headlight pods, mounted in cut-outs in the corners of the front lid, were raised and lowered by electric motors, actuated by relays when the headlights were switched on. In case of failure the pod motors had a manual operation facility, via a knurled knob on the end of the motor.

Set into the front bumper face extremities on the Mondial 8 and QV models were rectangular amber/white (all amber for the US) direction/side light units, with alongside them rectangular daytime flasher lights. The headlight lenses of French market cars were yellow to meet their legislation.

US market cars had rectangular surface-mounted side marker lights, just above bumper level fore and aft of the front and rear wheel arches respectively. On European models there was a slim rectangular side repeater indicator above the bumper forward of the front wheel arch. Japanese market cars had a large amber side marker light in the same position on each front wing. The doors were fitted with 'door open' warning lights in the trailing edge.

Twin-headlight arrangement of Mondial 8, QV and 3.2 compared with rectangular homofocal unit of Mondial t.

MAJOR ELECTRICAL EQUIPMENT

Mondial 8

Battery	12V 66Ah
Alternator	Bosch 65A
Electronic ignition	Marelli MED802A (MED801A for US)
Coils	Marelli BAE 209B
Starter motor	Bosch 0.001.314.006
Sparking plugs	Champion N76Y or Bosch W6DS

Mondial QV

Battery	12V 66Ah
Alternator	Bosch 80A
Electronic ignition	Marelli MED803A (MED805A for US)
Coils	Marelli BAE209B
Starter motor	Bosch 0.001.314.006
Sparking plugs	Champion N6GY (N6GY, N6YC or Bosch W6DS for US)

Mondial 3.2

Battery	12V 66Ah
Alternator	Bosch 85A
Electronic ignition	Marelli MED 806A
Coils	Marelli AEI 500C
Starter motor	Bosch 0.001.110.004
Sparking plugs	Champion A-6G (12mm)

Mondial t

Battery	12V 66/70Ah
Alternator	Delco GM 105A or Nippondenso
Injection/ignition	Bosch Motronic 2.5 or 2.7[1]
Starter motor	Bosch
Sparking plugs	Champion A-6G (12mm)

[1] 2.7 from chassis numbers 86793 (coupé) and 86986 (cabriolet).

The rear light assembly was universal for all markets, and remained unchanged throughout the life of the model. As with the two-seater 308/328 series, the rear lights were twinned either side of the tail panel, their form and function being identical to those from the 308 GTBi/Si onwards. US 3.2 and t models had an additional high-level brake light, fitted within the cabin on coupés at the top centre of the rear window, but in a raised central pod on the engine lid of cabriolets. Number plate illumination was by two small rectangular units in the trailing edge of the rear boot lid. A pair of high-intensity rear fog lights was fitted in the end sections of the lower valance below the rear bumper on all models except those destined for the US, on which they were omitted.

SUSPENSION & STEERING

The general suspension arrangement for the Mondial series was virtually identical to that of its two-seater counterparts: independent all round with unequal length wishbones, coil springs, double-acting shock absorbers, and front and rear anti-roll bars. Spring

SHOCK ABSORBERS

Model	Make	Front	Rear
Mondial 8/QV/3.2	Koni	82P2069	82P2073
Mondial t	Bilstein	8A5-7006	BA5-7007

SUSPENSION SETTINGS

Model	Front toe-in	Front camber	Rear toe-in	Rear camber
Mondial 8 & QV	2-3mm	+0°10′ to –0°10′	3-4mm	–1°20′ to –1°40′
Mondial 3.2 (TR390 rim)	1.5-2.5mm	–0°20′ to –0°40′	2-3mm	–1°20′ to –1°40′
Mondial 3.2 (16in rim)	2-3mm	–0°30′ to –0°50′	2-3mm	–1°30′ to –1°50′
Mondial t	1.5-2.5mm	–0°20′ to –0°40′	3-4mm	–1°20′ to –1°40′

Castor angle was 5°30′ on all models except the t, on which it was 7°. All settings are applicable to a car in static laden condition: full tank of petrol, two persons on board, 20kg of luggage.

rates, shock absorber type and suspension settings were changed to suit the Mondial's extra weight and different weight distribution – details are given in the accompanying panels.

Suspension geometry on the 3.2 model was changed to provide anti-dive and zero offset to suit the ABS braking system, which was introduced, initially as an option, in 1987 and became standard in 1988. This resulted in revised track dimensions, front track increasing from 1495mm (58.8in) to 1520mm (59.8in) and rear track decreasing from 1517mm (59.7in) to 1510mm (59.4in).

The Mondial t featured electronically controlled shock absorbers to give a choice of three ride settings – hard, medium or soft – from a selector switch on the centre console. The system control unit monitored acceleration and deceleration relative to the setting; if they came outside a pre-set threshold, the unit selected an optimum fixed setting in the range, to minimise roll and pitch.

Steering was by rack and pinion on all models, the Mondial 8 and QV having 3.45 turns lock to lock and a turning circle of 12.5m (41ft). The 3.2 model had the same number of turns but a reduced – and more practical – turning circle of 11.85m (39ft), while the t model needed only 3 turns lock to lock to produce an 11m (36ft) turning circle. The collapsible steering column was adjustable for both height and reach. Steering ball joints were lubrication-free sealed-for-life units, with automatic slack take-up facility.

The Mondial t was provided with power-assisted steering from an engine-driven hydraulic pump mounted at the left-hand front corner of the engine block, with hydraulic lines to the hydraulic rack and pinion unit at the base of the steering column.

BRAKES

The braking systems used on the Mondials were parallel to those on the equivalent two-seater models, with ventilated discs all round and a tandem master cylinder feeding separate front and rear circuits, incorporating vacuum servo assistance. A dashboard warning light, which also served as the handbrake 'on' warning light, advised of a pressure loss in either of the two circuits.

On Mondial 8 and QV models there was a separate brake fluid reservoir mounted in the front compartment, but brake and clutch fluid reservoirs were integrated on the 3.2 and t models. The handbrake was cable-operated on the rear disc calipers on models up to QV chassis number 43011, all subsequent Mondials having separate handbrake shoes bearing on the inner surface of the rear disc brake hub. Ferodo brake pads were type I/D 346 GG on the Mondial 8, QV and 3.2, and type 3416F on the Mondial t.

ABS braking became available as an option on the 3.2 Mondial during 1987 and was standardised in 1988, this feature carrying through to the t models.

WHEELS & TYRES

Road wheels were cast light alloy, always with five-bolt fixing and five-spoke design, fitted with a circular yellow plastic hub centre cap bearing the *Cavallino Rampante*, and given a lacquered silver finish.

There were only two basic wheel patterns. The wheel fitted to the Mondial 8 and QV had a flat centre section with its own inner rim, the face being virtually in line with the main rim, and the spoke edges were raised and ribbed. The wheel for the 3.2 and t was a smoother design that had a convex profile with the spokes blending into the main rim.

Instead of a spare wheel, the Mondial t was supplied with a can of puncture repair solvent to re-inflate the tyre as a temporary measure, but a conventional spare wheel could be provided as an option.

Wheels fitted to Mondial 8 and QV models (facing page, left) had central spoked section almost in line with rim, whereas wheels on Mondial 3.2 and t models (right) had convex spokes.

WHEELS/TYRES

Model	Front wheels	Front tyres	Rear wheels	Rear tyres
Mondial 8 & QV	180TR 390	Michelin TRX 240/55 VR390	180TR 390	Michelin TRX 240/55 VR390
Mondial 3.2	180TR 390	Michelin TRX 220/55 VR390	180TR 390	Michelin TRX 240/55 VR390
	7Jx16	Goodyear Eagle 205/55 VR16 NO	8Jx16	Goodyear Eagle 225/55 VR16 NO
Mondial t	7Jx16	Goodyear Eagle 205/55 ZR16	8Jx16	Goodyear Eagle 225/55 ZR16
	7Jx16	Michelin MXX 205/55 ZR16	8Jx16	Michelin MXX 225/55 ZR16

IDENTIFICATION PLATES

All models had identification plates in standard locations, but, as noted in the chapter on the 308/328 models concurrently in production (see page 57), numerous legislation changes and differences world-wide produced a vast range of requirements for specific markets.

For the various Mondial models the standard identification labels were as follows:

Mondial 8 and QV

1 Engine type and number plate affixed to the centre of the engine block vee at the cam belt drive end.
2 Vehicle type and chassis number on the engine compartment upper right-hand chassis tube.
3 Homologation plate on the bulkhead of the front compartment on the right-hand side.
4 Vehicle type and chassis number on an aluminium plate on a steering column shroud upstand.
5 Tyre pressure recommendation label in the lower corner of the windscreen on the driver's side.
6 Engine and gearbox lubricants plate on the upper left-hand side of the engine bay.
7 Anti-freeze plate on the top of the cooling system header tank in the engine bay.
8 Paint label on the right-hand side of the inner surface of the rear luggage compartment frame.

Mondial 3.2

Label locations were exactly as on the Mondial 8 and QV, with the exception of the tyre pressure label which moved to the inside of the glovebox.

Mondial t

1 Engine type and number plate affixed to the centre of the block vee beneath the injection casting at the rear of the engine.
2 Vehicle type and chassis number on the engine compartment upper right-hand chassis tube.
3 Vehicle Identification Number (VIN) plate on the right-hand bulkhead of the front compartment. See page 126 for guidance about how to decode the useful VIN information.
4 Type approval plate alongside the VIN plate on front compartment bulkhead.
5 Dipped beam homologation label alongside the VIN plate on front compartment bulkhead.
6 Lubricant plate for coupé on upper left-hand side of the engine compartment. On the cabriolet it was affixed to the underside of the engine cover on the central shield plate.
7 Anti-freeze plate on the top of the cooling system header tank in the engine compartment.
8 Vehicle type and chassis number on an aluminium plate on a steering column shroud upstand.
9 Tyre pressure label on inner face of coupé central console compartment lid. This was fitted to the passenger door shut post on cabriolets.
10 Paint label on the right-hand side of the inner surface of the rear luggage compartment frame.
11 Screen washer type approval plate on the face of the washer reservoir bottle in the front compartment.
12 Ferrari identification plate on left-hand side of upper engine bay frame to bulkhead of passenger compartment.

As noted in the chapter on the 308/328 models (see page 57), there were numerous additional labels for specific markets, examples of some of these being provided in that chapter.

Vehicle Identification Number (VIN) stamped into upper right-hand chassis tube alongside engine compartment (above) and also on a plate fixed to steering column upstand (below) – last five digits give Ferrari chassis number.

PRODUCTION DATA

Model	Production period	Chassis number range	Number built
Mondial 8 coupé	1980-82	31075-41727	703
Mondial QV coupé	1982-85	41737-59131	1145
Mondial QV cabrio	1983-85	47247-59163	629
3.2 Mondial coupé	1985-89	58277-79671	987
3.2 Mondial cabrio	1985-89	59393-78895	810
Mondial t coupé	1989-93	79596-97698	858
Mondial t cabrio	1989-93	80339-97733	1017

348 SERIES (1989-95)

In 1989 348 replaced 328, although family resemblance is closer to Testarossa, particularly in straked door inlets to side-mounted radiators.

Announced in 1989 at the Frankfurt Salon, the 348 tb (Berlinetta) and 348 ts (Spider/targa) were the first completely new models from the company since the death of Enzo Ferrari in August 1988. These Pininfarina-designed replacements for the 328 series were radically different in appearance from their predecessors.

In looks they were more akin to a scaled-down Testarossa, with straked radiator intake panels in the door skins and rectangular rear light assemblies behind a matt black slatted grille. As on the Testarossa, the front grille with the traditional egg-crate effect was only a dummy to maintain a semblance of unity with the new family look.

As with the Mondial t announced earlier in the year, the engine was longitudinally mounted amidships, and mated to a transverse gearbox. This placement in a shorter wheelbase resulted in the loss of the rear boot compartment, although the relocation of the water radiator freed additional luggage space in the front compartment.

This model also heralded another major departure from normal Ferrari practice. Gone was the traditional tubular chassis, replaced by a pressed steel one with a tubular engine sub-frame at the rear. The method of body assembly also changed, from a high degree of human input to assembly by computer-controlled welding machines at the ex-Scaglietti body plant in Modena.

At the time of the 348's announcement, the world was in the grip of 'car investment fever' and Ferraris were among the most sought-after cars of all. Whatever they were, new or old, there just were not enough Ferraris to satisfy demand from investment entrepreneurs trying to cash in on the market boom. From the time of its announcement, therefore, the 348 generated healthy order books and long waiting lists, until the market collapsed in the early 1990s.

Suddenly there was an excess of supply over demand, a situation not unique to Ferrari, which saw the demise of some manufacturers and severe financial problems for others. People took off their rose-tinted spectacles when looking at anything carrying the *Cavallino Rampante* and decided that perhaps the 348 was not 'the best thing since sliced bread', and that it did have its faults and shortcomings, notably nervous handling at high speed which did not instil confidence in the average driver. Couple this to a world-wide trade depression, and it is not difficult to see that sales were difficult for Ferrari at this time. Late in the relatively brief existence of the 348, further special editions and derivatives were introduced to breathe new life into the model.

Early in 1993 a special edition model called the

The tb (above) differs from ts (right) only in having a fixed roof. The 't' in model designation indicates race-derived novelty of transverse gearbox, while 'b' or 's' defines berlinetta or spider (targa), as on earlier models. Giallo Fly paintwork on these two examples shows to good effect matt black 'skirt' that distinguished tb/ts versions from renamed GTB/GTS pair that followed in 1993. German-registered tb poses with two-wheeled 'yellow peril', while ts shows US-spec identifying points – high-level brake light set into engine lid and faired-in side marker lights.

Removal of roof certainly did not spoil appearance of 348 Spider – in fact many enthusiasts prefer topless lines. Only difference between European (above) and US (left) models is in lighting on body flanks, with front indicator repeaters for former and front and rear side markers for latter.

Rear three-quarter comparison of UK-registered 348 Spider shows that Pininfarina put in a great deal of thought, as with Mondial cabriolet, to make soft-top look right as well as being practical to use.

From front three-quarter angle, only visual difference between later 348 GTB/GTS and earlier 348 tb/ts models is chromed Cavallino Rampante gracing front grille and body colour extending down to car's base line, matt black lower perimeter having been abandoned. From rear, appropriate badging and substitution of a chromed Cavallino Rampante for a black one are differences. To confuse the issue, however, some tb/ts models have been updated to GTB/GTS style, so only way to confirm identity is to check chassis number.

OPTIONAL EQUIPMENT

Metallic paintwork
Fitted leather luggage, by Schedoni

Sales of 348 Serie Speciale were confined to the US and only 100 examples were built, all in 1993. From this angle, this limited edition model's unique leather sports seats can be seen.

'Serie Speciale' was produced for the North American market, limited to 100 cars, though only 80 were produced, each with a numbered plaque on the door post. The significant differences were uncovered rear lights, a reprofiled front spoiler in body colour, the absence of matt black paint around the base of the main bodywork, an increase in rear track, and leather sports seats similar in design to those in the F40.

The Serie Speciale gave Maranello Concessionaires Ltd the idea of a limited edition model for the British market, and with the approval of the factory, this was made available. As with the Serie Speciale, the external modifications comprised the extension of the main body colour to the base of the car, thus eliminating the black finish for sills, front spoiler and lower rear valance, and the addition of a discreet body colour lip spoiler to the front. Internally a black suede Challenge steering wheel replaced the standard item, and drilled pedal pads were provided. Mechanically the only alteration was the provision of a sports exhaust system with reduced back pressure and a deeper note. Only four cars eventually received this treatment, their chassis numbers being 94421, 94621, 95304 and 95618.

In February 1993, a true Spider version was added to the range to provide a full convertible. This was announced on Rodeo Drive in Los Angeles, the heart of the main target sales area. As with the Mondial cabriolet, the soft-top line echoed the shape of the closed version.

Another offering for 1993 resulted from the introduction of the Challenge Race Series. For a set sum customers received a safety/performance kit and track support for a pan-European series of races, culminating with a final at the factory-owned Mugello circuit in October. After their racing career these Challenge cars could be easily returned to road form, although they should be identifiable by the roll cage fixing holes in the cabin section.

At the Frankfurt Salon in October 1993, the tb and ts badge suffixes were replaced by GTB and GTS, the only visual difference being the loss of the matt black

Main visual differences of US-only Serie Speciale from mainstream counterparts are uncovered tail light treatment with small central grille bearing a chromed Cavallino Rampante, and extra lip on front spoiler.

European market also received its own limited edition, in 1994, but this time with only 50 examples built: 348 GT Competizione had unique split-rim wheels and enamel Scuderia Ferrari shields on front wings, but head-on it looks no different from standard production cars.

finish for the front spoiler, the body sides below the doors and the lower rear valance, all now being finished in the body colour.

A European market 'Competizione' model was announced in 1994. This was a limited edition of 50 cars, though eventually 56 were produced, 8 of which were right-hand drive. These featured split-rim wheels with a different spoke design, enamel Scuderia Ferrari shields on the front wings, and interior embellishments. These cars should not be confused with the 348 GT Competizione that was developed and run in the Italian Supercar GT series in 1993 by the Jolly Club team, ending the season as Group 2 victor. Eleven of these racing models were produced, purely for development and track purposes, and a further two cars designated 348 GT/C-LM were specifically built for the 1994 Le Mans 24-hour race. The chassis numbers of these racing versions are given in the 'Production Data' table on page 97.

The 348 GTB and GTS continued in production until they were replaced by the F355 Berlinetta and GTS, which were presented at the March 1994 Geneva Salon. The 348 Spider continued in production alongside the F355 models, until the F355 Spider was launched consecutively in Monte Carlo and Los Angeles (on Rodeo Drive again) in April 1995.

During the whole production period the only visual differences on US versions were the flush side marker lights in the front and rear wings and a central high-level brake light in the trailing edge of the engine lid.

Body & Chassis

The 348 model was the first road-going Ferrari to utilise a unitary construction chassis/body assembly, albeit with a separate tubular engine/gearbox subframe bolted to the main chassis unit, its intention being to simplify engine/gearbox removal for maintenance or repair.

With world-wide legislation on crash tests having become more stringent and homogeneous during the 1980s, the chassis of the 348 was designed to meet all world requirements and impact absorbency was built into the package. Thus there were no protruding bumpers of heavier section for US cars, as there had been on earlier models.

The complete front and central chassis unit was formed from box-section steel, with steel bulkhead and floor panels welded to the main frame. To this frame were welded the windscreen surround, rear buttresses and roof section (coupé) or rear roof panel (spider). The spider featured strengthening gussets on the door hinge and shut posts, together with heavier gauge steel sill panels to offset the reduction in rigidity inherent in a convertible body unit.

Most of the body panels were also steel pressings, the exceptions being aluminium for the front and rear lids, and glass-fibre for the front and rear body/bumper sections and sill panels, all of which were bolted to the main chassis. The front wings were retained by bolts to the chassis and three additional tack welds, while the rear wings were fully welded. The construction of the 348 GT Competizione was a little more sophisticated, with the door panels, sill covers and front and rear body/bumper units made of a Kevlar and carbon-fibre composite material.

The vinyl-look moulded plastic roof panel of the ts/GTS model was located by two pins into the rear roof section, and retained at the front by a pair of catches on the windscreen rail. As on previous versions, the roof section could be stowed behind the seats when not in use. Roof panel supports were provided in this location, together with a protective cover fixed to the rear bulkhead.

The front grille was aesthetic only, being a non-functional indent in the solid front panel, with a traditional matt black egg-crate grille in the recess. On the left side of the grille recess was a removable plug, giving access to a screwed socket in the chassis frame into which the towing eye-bolt (in the tool kit) could be fitted.

Sound and heat insulation panels were fitted to all inside surfaces of the cabin section, and, in the case of the engine/cabin bulkhead, to both engine and cabin sides. On the underside of the car a bolted section was provided along the base of the central tunnel to give access to the heater tubes, gearchange cables and hydraulic pipes.

There were no physical differences between the 348 tb/ts models and the 348 GTB/GTS models, apart from the new versions having the paint colour continue down to the base of the body, replacing the base-line black spoiler section, sill and lower rear panel of the earlier models. All Spiders had this full body colour feature. The Spider's canvas soft-top was manually operated, and retained by catches on the windscreen rail when closed; the vinyl or (optional) leather cover provided to conceal the folded soft-top was retained by snap fasteners.

Dimensions & Weights

Overall length	4230mm (166.5in)
Overall width	1894mm (74.6in)
Overall height	1170mm (46.1in)
Wheelbase	2450mm (96.4in)
Front track	1502mm (59.1in)
Rear track (except US SS)	1578mm (62.1in)
Rear track (US SS)	1628mm (64.1in)
Dry weight, coupé (EU)	1393kg (3071lb)
Dry weight, coupé (US)	1478kg (3258lb)
Dry weight, targa (EU)	1398kg (3082lb)
Dry weight, targa (US)	1483kg (3269lb)
Dry weight, spider (EU)	1370kg (3020lb)
Dry weight, spider (US)	1455kg (3207lb)

Note These are the most reliable figures from factory literature, but should be taken as a guide only since different figures are quoted in other factory sources.

Badge styles for all the varieties of 348.

Neat door push and lock arrangement: door is opened by pushing recess with a thumb and hooking fingers under top edge of door intake duct. Door mirror style did not change throughout the range.

Body Colours

Solid colours	Code
Bianco	FER 100
Giallo	FER 102
Nero	FER 1240
Rosso Corsa	FER 300/9

Metallic colours	Code
Argento	FER 101/C
Oro Chiaro	FER 104/C
Rosso	FER 305/C
Prugna	FER 306/C
Blu Chiaro	FER 503/C
Blu Sera	FER 504/C
Azzuro	FER 505/C
Blu Medio	FER 506/C
Verde Chiaro	FER 602/C
Verde Scuro	FER 603/C
Verde Tenue	FER 604/C
Grigio	FER 700/C
Marrone	FER 800/C
Nero	FER 901/C

Leather Upholstery Colours

Colour	Code
Rosso	A3171
Crema	A3997
Pale Grey	A4301
Grigio	A4302
Pale Blue	A4303
Charcoal	A4304
Dark Green	A4305
Sabbia	A4306
Dark Blue	A4307
Black	A8500

Carpet Colours

Colour	Code
Nero	80
Rosso	81
Testa di Moro	83
Blu	84
Bruciato	85

The Serie Speciale for the US market differed bodily in having a reprofiled front spoiler with a lip on the front edge, uncovered rear lights, and full body colour before it had been adopted as standard. The 348 GT Competizione for the European market was different only in having Kevlar inner sill cover panels.

Body Trim & Fittings

There were very few trim adornments to the smooth body envelope, and the general theme of the details was matt black rather than bright.

All glass surrounds had a matt black finish, as did the windscreen wipers; these parked to the right on left-hand drive cars, and to the left with right-hand drive. A pair of electrically operated door mirrors in body colour casings were provided on long, angled arms that projected from matt black support panels in the front edge of the door glass area. Door catches were oval push buttons in body colour, with the matt black lock barrel face above them, near the trailing edge above the side intake louvre panel; the top of this panel acted as a finger pull.

The rear lights were sited behind a full-width five-bar grille finished in matt black. The *Cavallino Rampante* in the centre had a matt black anodised finish on tb and ts models, but a chrome version appeared on the GTB/S and Spider models – and for these an identical emblem was added to the dummy front grille. The only exception to this rear-end trim was on the US Serie Speciale, which had uncovered rear lights and a chrome *Cavallino Rampante* on a small grille between them.

Other badging comprised a rectangular Ferrari shield on the front lid, 'Disegno di Pininfarina' badges on the lower body sides just ahead of the rear wheel arches, and a chrome Ferrari script badge on the rear top edge of the engine cover. The model description badges – 348 tb, 348 ts, 348 GTB, 348 GTS and 348 Spider – were on the right-hand rear face of the engine cover lid in black script with a central white rib. GT Competizione models had a surface-mounted enamel Scuderia Ferrari shield – an emblem traditionally reserved for racing Ferraris – on each front wing near the base of the windscreen pillar, and a '348 GT Competizione' badge on the tail. The race-prepared 348 Challenge cars were provided with a '348 Challenge' script badge in similar style to the GT Competizione and Spider versions.

On all models the fuel filler was behind a hinged flap on the left-hand rear wing, and fed an aluminium tank sited between the engine and passenger compartment. The front luggage compartment lid was released by a chromed lever on the driver's side inner wheel arch, a similar lever nearby on the inner sill giving access to the engine bay.

Paintwork

The range of factory colours manufactured by Glasurit was unchanged throughout the life of the series. These solid (standard) and metallic (optional) colours are listed in the accompanying table, together with their codes.

On 348 tb/s models the front spoiler section, sill panels, lower rear tail panel and the solid section of the engine cover were finished in matt black. With the introduction of the 348 GTB/S these features all became body colour, an update that initially had been introduced on the US limited edition Serie Speciale.

Interior Trim & Fittings

The interior trim and equipment layout was constant on the different models in the range and throughout the period of production, apart from on the two limited edition models and those cars modified to Challenge race-prepared specification.

Seats and interior panels were trimmed in leather. The seats were provided with deep bolsters on the squab and backrest, together with adjustable head restraints. Seat adjustment for fore/aft movement was by a bar under the front edge of the squab, and for backrest rake by a lever on the outer bottom edge that also permitted the back to tilt forward for access to the space behind. Lap and diagonal inertia reel seat belts were standard.

Along with a racing harness, the Challenge race kit included Kevlar seat shells covered in red cloth and featuring deep side bolsters extending into the head restraints. Similar seats were fitted to the GT Competizione and Serie Speciale, the latter having them trimmed in leather, but both of these limited edition models retained normal inertia reel seat belts.

The floor, inner wheel arches, lower door panels and rear bulkhead were carpeted. The roof lining and rear screen surrounds on coupé and targa models were covered initially with plain beige cloth, and later with a fine brown/beige or black/grey stripe cloth. The vinyl dashboard top and leather centre section of the door panel that extended from it were normally black, but customers could specify any other colour from the range if they desired – but again the factory did not recommend this due to the screen reflection problems that other colours created.

The steering wheel was a three-spoke design with the rim trimmed in leather, and the triangulated centre section housed the traditional horn push bearing a *Cavallino Rampante* on a yellow background. The GT Competizione, however, had a unique steering wheel with the limited edition serial number inscribed on it. The steering column on all models could be adjusted for height by a lever in the lower underside of the shroud. To the left of the column were two stalks, the longer one for lights and the shorter one for direction indicators. A stalk on the right of the column operated the windscreen washers and two-speed (plus intermittent) wipers.

Interior of 348 Spider (top) is typical of whole series, except for two limited edition models. Family likeness to previous V8-powered Ferraris is strong, but almost every detail is different. Fire extinguisher is non-standard safety precaution added by owner. Door detail (above) shows bodywork bulk required to incorporate intake duct to side-mounted radiators, and more avant-garde style for interior trim. Interior of Europe-only limited-edition 348 GT Competizione (right) featured lightweight Kevlar for seat shells (covered in red cloth to imitate F40) and sill panels. Special steering wheel (far right) carried appropriate script and serial number (out of 50) below crossed flags.

Interior of US-only 348 Serie Speciale shows deep-bolstered, leather-covered, Kevlar-framed seats unique to the model. Note belt catches passing through apertures in seat, and special dashboard plaque above centre console.

The handbrake was sited on the outside of the driver's seat. A small panel on the driver's door, forward of the pull section, contained switches for both electric windows and a lever to adjust the external mirrors, with a left or right selector switch below it. Electric heating for the mirrors was activated when the heated rear window was switched on.

Radio speakers were provided in the door panels and in the dashboard extremities, next to the directional air vents. A further pair of directional air vents was located in the centre of the dashboard, between the instrument nacelle and glovebox. The glovebox had a lift-up lid on the upper face of the dashboard, and contained an interior light with a plug-in auxiliary light socket.

Coupé and targa models had an interior light module at the rear of the roof section, comprising a square interior light actuated by door switches, with

an overriding off switch, and a directional spotlight with on/off switch adjacent. The Spider had a similar arrangement between the sun visors, which on all models featured a vanity mirror on the passenger's side. The dipping interior mirror was fixed to the windscreen by an adhesive pad. Plain glass was fitted all round, the front screen having a heavily tinted band across the top with the radio aerial embedded in it.

Air conditioning operating through the ventilation system was standard throughout the range. The compressor was mounted in the engine bay, belt-driven off the engine.

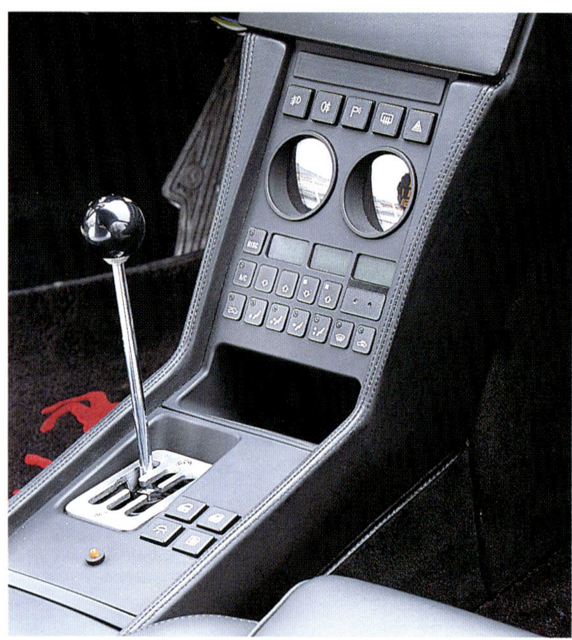

Close-up of instrument panel shows orange-on-black Veglia-Borletti dials with easy-to-define white/orange needles. Switchgear and two more dials – for oil temperature and fuel – were housed in neat centre console; gear lever changed sides for right-hand drive.

DASHBOARD & INSTRUMENTS

The main instrument nacelle protruded from the top of the dash panel, as it had done on the preceding range of two-seater V8 models. The face of the instrument panel was matt black, and the layout comprised banks of warning lights, down the sides and across the bottom, surrounding recessed black dials with fluorescent orange characters and needles.

On the left was the 320kph or 200mph speedometer incorporating distance recorder and trip meter. In the centre were two smaller dials, for oil pressure (upper) and water temperature (lower). On the right was the 10,000rpm rev counter with a solid orange segment marked from 7500rpm.

Other instruments were sited in the centre console that swept down at an angle from the lower dash panel, becoming horizontal just forward of the gear lever. Along the top edge of this console was a bank of five warning lights, with the relative push-button switches immediately below them; these controlled, from left, front fog lights, rear fog lights (where mandatory), parking lights, heated rear window and hazard warning lights. Below these was a pair of recessed circular dials for oil temperature (left) and fuel (right). Under these came a bank comprising, from left, a push-button switch for automatic heating control, selected temperature display, air flow display and electronic clock. The next row of six switches controlled, from left, automatic air conditioning, air temperature decrease/increase, fan speed decrease/increase and clock adjustment. Beneath these was a further row of seven push buttons for ventilation permutations – outside air intake, air to low level, air to low/mid level, air to mid level only, air to low level plus screen, demisting vents only and outside/recirculation air flap.

At the angle to the horizontal section was an uncovered oddments tray, behind which was the open-gate gear lever on the driver's side. This had a chrome shaft surmounted by a black plastic ball in which gear positions were inscribed in white. On the passenger side of the gate was a bank of three push-button switches controlling door locking, door unlocking, fuel filler flap release, plus a fourth 'dummy' switch. There then followed a short panel, an ashtray containing a cigarette lighter and a slotted holder for loose change. Right at the back of the console was a lockable glovebox on coupé and targa models, but only a recessed oddments tray on the Spider version.

LUGGAGE COMPARTMENT

With the move from transverse to longitudinal engine alignment, the rear luggage compartment of the 348's predecessors disappeared. The front compartment now became the only place for storage, apart from some space behind the seats.

However, luggage capacity here was much greater than on previous models, for two reasons. First, there was no longer a front-mounted water radiator and associated ducting to take up space. Second, the front and rear wheels were of different widths, as with the Mondial 3.2 and t models, so Ferrari provided a

TOOL KIT

- Puncture repair/inflator canister
- Alternator drive belt
- Towing eye bolt
- Set of 6-19mm open-end spanners
- Phillips screwdriver
- Universal pliers, 180mm
- Spark plug spanner with ratchet
- Spare bulbs
- Spare fuses
- Plug-in emergency light

compressed air repair/inflator canister instead of a conventional or spacesaver spare wheel.

As a result, the luggage well between the front wheels was a deep box, virtually square in shape and fully carpeted, with the leather tool kit bag secured to one side; the tools themselves are listed in the panel on the facing page. As with other models in the Ferrari range, a set of leather luggage manufactured by Schedoni was available as an option, to maximise the use of the available space. Covered sections around the wheel intrusions and across the passenger compartment bulkhead housed the fuse/relay board, washer bottle, wiper motor, brake and clutch master cylinders and reservoir, ABS braking electronics, air horn compressor and power steering unit.

Twin air horns were fitted in the left-hand space forward of the wheel arch, which was occupied by the air conditioning condenser coil on the right-hand side, fed by an intake in the front spoiler and exhausting through slots into the wheel arch. The battery and isolator switch were located at the front of the compartment, and separated cavities housed the retractable headlights and their motors.

Unlike previous two-seater models, 348's longitudinal engine location forbids a rear luggage compartment, so spare wheel is sacrificed in order to provide reasonable space under front lid, helped by all cooling system arrangements now being at rear. Packaging is very neat; tan leather case, just visible, contains tool kit.

ENGINE

Whereas all the two-seater mainstream production V8 predecessors had transverse engines, the 348 received a longitudinally aligned variant of the 90° V8, with capacity increased to 3405cc (207.8cu in). The new engine, coded F119D, had bore and stroke dimensions of 85mm (3.35in) × 75mm (2.95in), a compression ratio of 10.4:1 and four valves per cylinder.

Claimed power output was 300bhp at 7200rpm with maximum torque of 238lb ft at 4200rpm. This engine also saw a return to dry-sump lubrication, a feature shared by the concurrent Mondial t, and was mated to a new transverse gearbox fitted to the rear of the engine, with the flywheel and clutch on the end of the gearbox. This new configuration allowed the whole assembly to be fitted lower in the chassis, lowering the car's centre of gravity.

The cylinder heads and block were constructed from light alloy, with Nikasil-coated steel bore liners in direct contact with the coolant. The heads continued to feature twin overhead camshafts per bank actuating twin inlet and exhaust valves, with a centrally located spark plug for each cylinder. The camshafts were driven by a single toothed belt via pulleys and a tensioner from a geared wheel, chain-driven off the crankshaft front end.

The crankshaft was steel and ran in five main bearings, with a shaft to the rear transmitting power to the flywheel at the rear of the gearbox. On the front end was a gear wheel that drove the oil pump in the sump and the camshaft drive gear via chains. Keyed and bolted to the front end of the crankshaft was the main pulley, from which drive was taken via a multi-grooved belt to the alternator and water pump, with a separate belt serving the air conditioning compressor mounted on the right-hand side of the engine. The water pump was mounted at the front centre of the vee and the alternator on the bottom left-hand front side with a heat shield above it. The starter motor was mounted towards the back of the car, on the upper right-hand side of the clutch/flywheel housing at the rear of the gearbox.

The pairs of inlet and exhaust valves were arranged at an angle of 32° 30′ with respect to each other, actuated by bucket tappets and clearance adjustment shims from the camshafts. Timing data is given in the panel below.

TIMING DATA

Inlets open BTDC	14°
Inlets close ABDC	53°
Exhausts open BBDC	53°
Exhausts close ATDC	10°

Valve timing should be measured with a clearance of 0.50mm (0.020in) between the tappet thimbles and camshaft. Valve clearances with cold engine should be 0.20-0.25mm (0.008-0.010in) for inlet valves and 0.35-0.40mm (0.014-0.016in) for exhaust valves, measured between the valve pads and camshaft. Firing order is 1-5-3-7-4-8-2-6.

SYSTEM CAPACITIES (LITRES)

Model	Fuel	Cooling	Washer	Engine oil	Gearbox oil
All models except Spider	95	20	3	11	4
Spider	88	20	3	11	4

Engine bay with longitudinal V8 was identical on all 348 models, and dominated as usual by injection intake casting and associated air ducting. Aluminium foil panel in foreground is exhaust silencer heat shield.

A Bosch Motronic combined injection/ignition system was fitted to all cars, the exact specification changing from M2.5 to M2.7 at chassis numbers 86406 (tb) and 86407 (ts). This sophisticated system monitored the fuel quantity and ignition advance required to optimise engine efficiency, relative to engine speed and air intake volume. Much of the equipment was mounted in the centre of the vee, each cylinder bank having its own electronic control unit, individual fuel pump (mounted in the base of the tank), coil and power module (sited on the side of the engine bay). The injector manifolds took air from a centrally mounted air filter box sited over the gearbox, and this in turn drew air through ducts from intakes sculpted into the rear buttresses, behind the side windows.

The cooling system comprised twin radiators, each fitted with a thermostatically controlled fan, mounted either side of the engine bay and fed with air from the door intake grilles. The radiator on the right was smaller, as the lower portion of its opening was occupied by an oil cooler with its own thermostatically controlled fan. Coolant was fed through the radiators via piped connections to the water pump, with a branch connection to the header tank mounted on the right of the engine bay.

A fabricated steel exhaust collector manifold was provided for each bank of cylinders. This took the gases via catalytic converters (where fitted in the horizontal pipe from each bank) to the upper of two horizontal silencer boxes across the rear of the car. The gases passed from the upper to the lower box through a pair of pipes, and from there to atmosphere through a pair of chromed tail-pipe assemblies that exited through cut-outs in the lower edge of the rear valance. Catalytic converters were not introduced on cars for mainstream European markets until the provi-

OVERALL GEAR RATIOS

	tb/ts (non-cat)	tb/ts (cat)	GTB/S (EU)	GTB/S (US)
First	1:12.078	1:12.517	1:13.017	1:13.982
Second	1:7.910	1:8.198	1:8.524	1:9.158
Third	1:5.480	1:5.676	1:5.906	1:6.343
Fourth	1:4.110	1:4.260	1:4.429	1:4.757
Fifth	1:3.236	1:3.354	1:3.393	1:3.644
Reverse	1:10.467	1:10.847	1:11.282	1:12.118
Diff spur ratio	16/55	16/57	16/57	16/57

sion of Bosch Motronic M2.7 injection/ignition from chassis number 86406 (tb) and 86407 (ts). Earlier cars without catalytic converters could run on either leaded or unleaded fuel.

Exhaust gas test points were provided on the manifolds and on the main pipes to the catalysers/silencers. All US, Swiss, Austrian and Swedish market 348s were fitted with catalytic converters, which were progressively introduced to other markets as dictated by changes in legislation. US cars were also fitted with an evaporative emission control system on the fuel storage and filter system: this comprised a sealed filler cap and a charcoal canister mounted in the engine bay, along with a fluid/vapour separating manifold, a purge valve and a two-way valve incorporating a roll-over safety device.

Lighting on 348 is neat, with pop-up homofocal headlight unit and – for first time since 308 GT4 – all rear light functions gathered into a single cluster, seen fully exposed on US limited-edition 348 Serie Speciale; on all other models these lights were shielded, rather impractically, by a five-bar matt black grille.

Transmission

Along with the engine placement, the transmission arrangement was the biggest mechanical difference from the preceding models. The gearbox and final drive assembly was housed in a single unit mounted on the rear of the engine, with the flywheel and clutch unit on the rear of the gearbox.

The design of this powertrain evolved from the transmission developed in 1974-75 for the 312T Formula 1 car, which also had a longitudinal engine and transverse gearbox. This configuration – *trasversale* in Italian – gave the F1 car its T suffix and explains the t in the 348's original tb and ts model suffixes.

Power was transmitted from the engine to the dry clutch/flywheel assembly via a shaft running through the gearbox. On this was mounted an idler gear wheel that meshed with one below it on the gearbox primary shaft. This transmitted the power back to the gearbox main shaft, mounted at right angles across the car (hence *trasversale*), via a crown wheel and pinion.

Parallel with the main shaft, and just forward of it, was the lay shaft, the individual gears being a combination of the meshing gear wheels and synchronisers on these two shafts, apart from reverse gear which was driven off the main shaft via an intermediate gear, to change direction of motion, to the lay shaft. The order of the individual gears along these shafts from right to left was second, third, reverse, first, fifth and fourth. From the lay shaft power was transmitted via a pair of bevel gears to the limited slip differential (mounted immediately above the main and lay shafts) and thence to the drive shafts, which were bolted to the differential output flanges on either side of the transmission casing.

Gear selection from the central lever inside the cabin was via a pair of cables running through the central tunnel under the engine, to a selector mechanism that transmitted the motion via internal shafts to the gear selector forks.

The clutch was an 8.5in diameter dry type, on a 'bimass' flywheel with an internal oscillation damper, hydraulically operated via the pedal master cylinder and slave cylinder on the clutch casing that actuated the release mechanism.

The gearbox/differential was housed in a ribbed aluminium casing, with a matching cover for the clutch/flywheel assembly bolted to the rear and featuring the *Cavallino Rampante* on the centre rear and Ferrari script along the lower edge.

Electrical Equipment & Lights

The electrical system was 12-volt negative earth, served from a 66Ah or 70Ah battery fed by a Delco GM 105A alternator on early cars or a Nippondenso on later models owing to its improved reliability and performance.

MAJOR ELECTRICAL EQUIPMENT

Battery	12V 66/70Ah
Alternator	Delco GM 105A or Nippondenso
Injection/ignition	Bosch Motronic M2.5 or M2.7[1]
Starter motor	Bosch (factory part number 134387)
Sparking plugs (EU)	Champion A-6G (12mm)
Sparking plugs (US)	Bosch X4CS or XR4CS

[1] The change from M2.5 to M2.7 occurred at chassis numbers 86406 (tb) and 86407 (ts).

SUSPENSION SETTINGS

Model	Front toe-in	Front camber	Rear toe-in	Rear camber
All standard models	1mm +/– 0.5mm	0° to +0°20′	2.5-3.0mm	–1°30′ to –1°50′
348 GT Competizione	2.0-3.0mm	–0°30′ to –0°50′	2.5-3.5mm	–1°20′ to +1°40′

Castor angle is a constant 5°30′ +/– 0°15′. These figures are applicable to a car in static laden condition: full tank of petrol, two persons on board. These are guide figures only as the factory issued several bulletins quoting different settings for improved handling: it is advisable to check with an approved dealer to obtain the correct values for a specific car.

As with the Mondials, the lighting was designed to cater for as many world markets as possible within a standard specification, making all market models very similar in appearance. The US side marker lights on the 348 series were flush-mounted into the front and rear bumper/valance panels, making them so unobtrusive that they are almost unnoticeable on a red car in daylight. The US market mandatory high-level brake light was a slim, rectangular unit neatly flushed into the trailing edge of the engine cover. Japanese legislation still required amber side marker lights on the front wings only. Obviously different markets necessitated different dipping arrangements, bulb wattage, and lens colours, such as amber front sidelights on US models and yellow headlights for France.

The headlights were slim, rectangular, homofocal units identical to those on the Mondial t, with dipped beam in the outer part of the unit and main beam in the inner section. As on the Mondials, they were housed in retractable pods in the corners of the front lid, and were raised and lowered automatically when the lights were switched on, via electric motors that had manual back-up operation.

In the front bumper unit on either side of the grille were integral units containing side lights, indicators, daytime flashers and fog lights. European cars had small, circular, amber indicator repeaters mounted on the front wings, just above the central body crease line and between wheel arch and door.

At the rear was a pair of slim, rectangular light units mounted behind a matt black grille with horizontal slats that extended the full width of the tail panel, above the bumper unit. The exception to this arrangement was the Serie Speciale, which had exposed light units with a small central grille between them. Each light unit contained, from the outer edge, an amber direction indicator, brake light, reflector and high-intensity fog light, and above these was a rear/parking light strip with a reversing light at the inner end.

SUSPENSION & STEERING

The general suspension arrangement for the 348 series followed Ferrari's standard practice for the previous models: independent all round, with pressed steel wishbones, coil springs, double-acting shock absorbers, and front and rear anti-roll bars. The front suspension geometry was designed to provide anti-dive and zero offset for the improved stability that is essential when ABS is fitted.

Shock absorbers were gas-filled Bilstein units, with factory code 141857 (front) and 141858 (rear) up to assembly number 8798, thereafter 146290 (front) and 146291 (rear). At the front the shock absorber/spring assembly was positioned between the wishbones, whereas at the rear the unit was above the wishbones to accommodate the drive shafts. Guide values for camber angle and toe-in for front and rear wheels on all models are shown in the panel.

Steering was rack and pinion, via a collapsible column and height-adjustable steering wheel. The wheel needed three turns lock to lock to provide a turning circle of 11.85m (39ft). The system was sealed for life and maintenance-free, with automatic slack take-up facility.

BRAKES

The 348 models employed ventilated discs to each road wheel, with a twin-circuit hydraulic system (one each for front and rear brakes), servo assistance via a hydraulic multiplier, front/rear pressure regulator and a Teves Mark II ABS system.

ABS is activated automatically above 5mph if a wheel locks, through an electronic control unit mounted in the front compartment. A sensor on each wheel hub sends signals back to this control unit, which processes information received and if necessary energises hydraulic circuit solenoid valves to adjust pressure in the systems. The driver can detect ABS operation by pulses through the brake pedal.

The ABS system was provided with a warning light in the main instrument panel that illuminates when the ignition is switched on, and then extinguishes if the system is functioning normally. If there is a failure, the light remains illuminated and the system is de-activated, leaving normal braking only. If the brake failure warning light is illuminated continuously at the same time, a lack of fluid or boost pressure is indicated and the car is unsafe to drive. ABS helps the car to be steered under braking, but does not necessarily help it to stop.

The handbrake was cable-operated on separate brake shoes that acted on the inner surfaces of the rear disc brake hubs. A 'handbrake on' warning light was

This five-spoke wheel design – yet another variation on a familar theme – was used on all 348s except for limited-edition GT Competizione.

provided in the main instrument panel. Brake pads were Galfer type 3318, those at the front incorporating sensors that illuminated the handbrake warning light when they reached a pre-set state of wear.

Wheels & Tyres

Road wheels were cast light alloy with five-bolt fixing and an aerodynamic five-spoke design unique to the 348 series, with the traditional yellow hub centre cap bearing the *Cavallino Rampante*. Due to the different front and rear rim widths, no spare wheel was provided. Instead there was a canister of compressed repair/inflator solvent in the tool kit.

The only exception to the standard wheel specification was on the GT Competizione, which was fitted with split-rim Speedline wheels featuring curved, ribbed spokes of a design similar to that used on Ferrari's 512 TR and 456 GT models. These wheels had a highly polished finish in plain lacquered aluminium, whereas the finish of the standard wheels was lacquered silver.

Wheels/Tyres

Model	Front wheels	Front tyres	Rear wheels	Rear tyres
All standard models	7.5Jx17	215/50 ZR17[1]	9Jx17	255/50 ZR17[1]
348 GT Competizione	8Jx18in	225/40 ZR18[2]	10Jx18	265/40 ZR18[2]

[1] Alternative makes were Pirelli P700Z or Bridgestone RE71, although 348 Serie Speciale (US only) came only with Pirelli P Zero. [2] Always Pirelli P Zero.

Identification Plates

The 348 series, in common with all Ferraris, had identification plates in standard locations, but again different markets requested certain information that sometimes had to be displayed in specific locations on the car. The normal European market labelling was as follows:

1 Engine type and serial number plate affixed to the centre of the block vee beneath the injection casting at the rear of the engine.
2 Vehicle type and chassis number on the chassis suspension support plate on the right-hand side of the engine bay.
3 Vehicle Identification Number (VIN) plate on the passenger side door hinge post. See page 126 for guidance about how to decode the useful VIN information.
4 Lubrication plate on the underside of the right-hand side of the engine cover.
5 Paint label on the underside of the centre rear section of the engine cover.
6 Anti-freeze plate on the top face of the radiator header tank on the right-hand side of the engine bay.
7 Ferrari identification plate on the chassis suspension support on the left-hand side of the engine bay.
8 Unleaded fuel label on inside of fuel filler opening cover flap.
9 Tyre pressure plate on underside of glovebox lid on centre tunnel, or on driver's door shut post on Spider.
10 Aluminium vehicle type and chassis number plate on steering column shroud upstand.
11 Dipped beam homologation label on forward right-hand side of front lid.
12 Screen washer type approval plate on top of the washer bottle in the front compartment.

US models had additional labels for an FMV Safety Standard certification plate on the door shuts and a VIN bar code label on the driver's door shut post, while on the underside of the engine cover there were labels for Vehicle Emission Control and Catalyst Information, plus a VEC bar code label. The tyre pressure label was fitted to the passenger's door shut post on all US models.

Although other markets had various labelling requirements, the foregoing covers the majority of models produced.

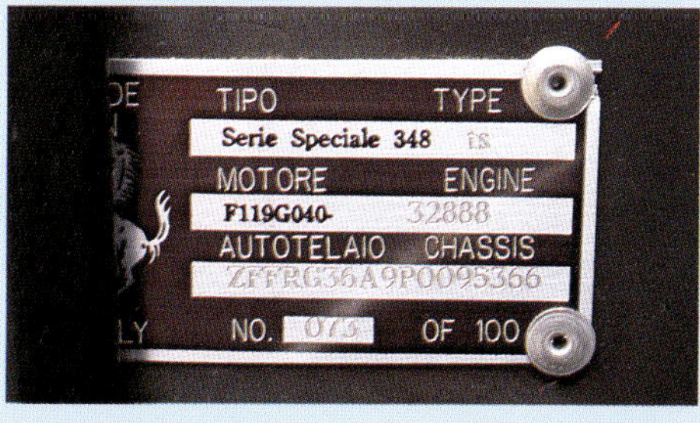

The 348 Serie Speciale had a special identity plate on door shut post.

Production Data

Model	Production period	Chassis number range	Number built
348 tb	1989-93	81617-96679	2894
348 ts	1989-93	81651-96964	4228
348 Serie Speciale (US)	1993	92812-95820	80
348 Spider	1993-95	94504-99947	1146
348 GTB	1993-94	96655-99697	222
348 GTS	1993-94	96824-99197	218
348 GT Competizione (EU)	1993-94	96064-99143	56

Note Thirteen cars were developed into racing versions. Eleven 348 GT Competizione derivatives had chassis numbers 84248, 95380, 96064, 96547, 97296, 97933, 98226, 98367, 98676, 99107 and 99143. Two 348 GT/C-LM derivatives specifically built for the 1994 Le Mans 24-hour race had chassis numbers 97553 and 98997.

288 GTO (1984-86)

In profile, 288 GTO's high-stalked door mirrors, triple rear wing slots (reminiscent of those on the front wings of a 250 GTO), highly polished split-rim wheels, deep tail spoiler and additional duct under the door are the most obvious clues that this is not a 308 GTB. The Ferrari factory only ever referred to the car as the GTO, although it is generally called the 288 GTO to differentiate it from the earlier 250 GTO model. The 288 addition is a reference to the cubic capacity of the engine, 2.8 litres, and the number of cylinders, eight."

The car from which the term 'supercar' emanated was unveiled to the public at the 54th Geneva Salon in 1984, after months of spy photographs in the world's motoring press and speculation as to what the heavily camouflaged models seen around Maranello actually were. In fact there was confusion for the outside world: at the same time Testarossa prototypes were sharing the roads of Emilia Romagna and that model was presented at the Paris Salon of the same year.

At a glance the 288 GTO looked rather like a 308 GTB on steroids, but apart from visual similarity it shared very little with that model. Some of the 288 GTO's styling features, in fact, had been displayed on a 308 GTB design exercise by Pininfarina shown at the 1977 Geneva Salon. These included a deeper front spoiler, increased wing volume, a more pronounced rear lip to the engine cover, front lid louvres for radiator exhaust, and quadruple driving lights.

Along with other Formula 1 constructors in the early 1980s, Ferrari had begun to use composite materials for racing car structures, and the 288 GTO was the first Ferrari production car to feature this new technology in its body panels and certain other areas, all in the interests of lightness. The GTO designation was inspired by a famous ancestor – the legendary 250 GTO of 1962-64.

The original concept for the model had been to produce a car that complied with FISA's Group B competition regulations. The construction of a minimum of 200 cars was required for Group B homologation – hence the O for *Omologata* in the GTO title. During the course of production the regulations changed, leaving no suitable racing class for the car. However, by then the die had been cast, and wealthy customers world-wide were clamouring to obtain an example of the fastest, most powerful, most charismatic and desirable production Ferrari of the period. Never mind that it would never turn a wheel in anger in competition...

Only one version was ever produced, with no market variations. Those bought by US customers, therefore, had to be acquired on a personal import basis, with legislation to federal standards the responsibility of the owner.

So strong was demand that the initial production target of 200 was increased to what most informed sources believe to be 272 examples, all of which were left-hand drive. Even then, there were people willing to pay a premium over the normal price, and some customers were selling contracts even before they had received their cars. This was the starting point for the crazy price spiral of the mid-to-late 1980s.

A development model was also produced, making

Three-quarter views amplify numerous differences between 288 GTO and transverse-engined V8 stablemates. Notable are quadruple driving lights, deep front spoiler, rear quarter bumpers, visible transmission casing, and a plethora of cooling slots for brakes, radiator and heat dissipation.

In your rear-view mirror, wide stance and quadruple driving lights give the game away…

…and, when it passes, subtle GTO logo on tail confirms your suspicions.

OPTIONAL EQUIPMENT

- Alternative interior trim: full leather or leather/cloth
- Air conditioning
- Electric windows
- Rear fog lights

even greater use of composite materials. The 288 Evoluzione was never a production car, although four of the five examples produced were sold to private collections. This model was basically a test bed for the next production model, the F40, which looked very different from the 288 GTO but evolved out of it.

Body & Chassis

In common with all Ferraris produced up to its date of introduction, the 288 GTO featured a separate tubular chassis frame of large oval-section steel tubes, with welded-on supplementary frames in square and rectangular section tubing for suspension, steering, door posts, body mounting and bumper supports.

The rear section of the main frame was bolted to the central unit through four pairs of square flanges, two per side, each secured by four bolts. This rear frame supported the engine, gearbox and rear suspension, the bolted flanges permitting removal of the complete assembly as one unit for maintenance.

The cockpit area incorporated a built-in tubular roll hoop contained in the door shut posts and within the roof headlining across the rear screen line. The cockpit floor pan was constructed in glass-fibre and bonded to the chassis tubes. The engine/cockpit bulkhead was a Kevlar-skinned aluminium honeycomb panel, with a removable centre section, constructed from Kevlar/Nomex composite, giving access to the front part of the engine.

The bodywork also incorporated a high degree of contemporary composite materials technology. The doors, wings, sills, lower front body section, rear valance and inner wheel arches were all glass-fibre mouldings. The upper front nose section between the wings, roof with rear buttresses, engine cover, and rear tail panel were constructed from a glass-fibre and Nomex composite material, while the front lid was a Kevlar/Nomex composite.

The louvres on the front lid, rear lid and front wings were aluminium painted body colour, while a natural-finish aluminium grille with horizontal slats sat in the front radiator inlet below the bumper. The lower front body section incorporated a deep spoiler with five slim horizontal slots under the radiator opening, and brake cooling inlets sculpted into the lower section at the outer extremities.

A threaded bush was provided at the right-hand front side of the chassis so that the towing eye (provided in the tool kit) could be screwed in if necessary. The location was between the bumper and inner auxiliary light in the radiator inlet.

Dimensions & Weights

Overall length	4225mm (166.3in)
Overall width	1850mm (72.8in)
Overall height	1150mm (45.3in)
Wheelbase	2450mm (96.4in)
Front track	1589mm (62.6in)
Rear track	1562mm (61.5in)
Dry weight	1160kg (2557lb)

Body Trim & Fittings

The body was virtually devoid of any bright trim. The door and side window frames were black anodised aluminium, with plain black rubber surrounds to the front and rear screens. Windscreen wipers had a matt black finish and parked to the right. Tinted glass was fitted all round, the windscreen featuring a heavily tinted band along the top.

One of the most prominent external features was the pair of door mirrors, their tall, vertical, body colour support columns required to provide the mandatory field of view over the bulbous rear wings. Each door had a circular chrome lock barrel above the indent line, with a matt black release catch on the upper trailing edge.

The left-hand rear wing had a hinged flap with finger recess over the fuel filler cap. A matching flap on the right-hand rear wing, with a cable release from the interior of the car, gave access to the oil catch tank filler cap. Behind the wheel arch on each rear wing were three raked slots with black diamond mesh on the inner face. These exhausted hot air from the engine bay, although their presence probably owed more to styling – they were a deliberate cue from the

Rear-hinged engine cover contains plenty of louvres to dissipate heat from twin-turbo engine; unlike transverse-engined models, buttresses do not form part of the lid. Rear quarter windows curve in to provide air intakes for cooling engine bay.

Door mirrors are mounted on tall stalks to improve visibility over rear spoiler, and, like matt black door release catches, are unique to GTO.

Recessed Scuderia Ferrari enamel shield – an emblem traditionally reserved for competition models – reveals that GTO originally had a higher purpose than satisfying whims of speculators. And tail panel badges reflecting autumn sun discreetly say it all...

front wing slots on the legendary 250 GTO – than to necessity. At the front of each rear wing, just below the matt black body indent line, was a rectangular aluminium 'Disegno di Pininfarina' badge.

Each front wing had an enamel Scuderia Ferrari shield near the upper trailing edge, mounted in a recess to provide a flush surface. The nose panel had a rectangular enamel Ferrari badge in the centre, while the four-bar aluminium grille below the bumper featured a chrome *Cavallino Rampante*. The rear tail panel had a GTO script badge on the right-hand side, in aluminium with a black centre strip to the lettering, and a black *Cavallino Rampante* to its right.

The front bumper was plain matt black, incorporating the side lights and turn indicators at its extremities. At the rear matching quarter bumpers were provided with a matt black panel for the registration plate mounting between them.

The engine lid was hinged on its rear edge, and retained at the front by circular chrome turn catches in the corners, with a central rectangular chrome lock and release lever assembly. The front lid was released by a chrome lever on the driver's side inner wheel arch, with an emergency pull ring below the dash panel for use in the event of cable failure.

On models for the German market, the buttress and rear wing intake scoops were fitted with black mesh screens to meet national legislation.

PAINTWORK

With the 288 GTO you could have any colour you liked as long as it was red – simple as that! The precise colour is Rosso Corsa FER 300/9. A 288 GTO in any other colour has been repainted since leaving the factory at Maranello.

The front and rear bumpers were matt black, and the indent line along the body sides between front and rear bumpers was painted matt black. The front screen posts were also finished in matt black to match and flow into the door window frames.

INTERIOR TRIM & FITTINGS

The choice of interior trim was almost as limited as the external colour, there being only two alternatives. Full black leather seats (code VM8500) were more usually specified, the alternative being black leather with the central squab and backrest panels in bright orange cloth. If cloth was chosen, the inset dash face panel on the passenger's side was finished in the same material. This panel also featured a small GTO script badge, of the same design as that on the tail panel.

The seats, assembled on Kevlar frames, had a retro aspect to the stitch pattern, as they looked virtually identical to those of the 365 GTB/4 Daytona. They

The two trim combinations for 288 GTO, both with Daytona-like 'buttoned' seat pleating. Most customers chose plain black leather, but orange cloth seat centres could also be specified; this rather garish scheme was echoed in passenger's side dashboard panel and driver's side oddments pocket. Colour highlighting apart, matt black flock material on dashboard was designed to minimise windscreen reflections. Inner door panel, like rest of the car, has nothing in common with V8 stablemates; even radio speaker, bearing its own yellow 'Ferrari GTO' badge, was specially produced.

were adjustable for fore/aft movement by a bar under the front of the squab, and for rake by a lever on the lower outside edge of the backrest. Three-point inertia reel seat belts were provided as standard, although some owners fitted full harness belts to give more positive support when driving enthusiastically.

The floor, inner sills, wheel arches and rear bulkhead were trimmed with black carpet – again there was no choice of colour. The dashboard was finished in a black suede-effect material to prevent reflections in the steeply raked screen. The roof lining and rear window surround were in a white perforated plastic.

The door panels contained elasticated map pockets in the lower portion, with the door release catch just forward of them. On cars with manually operated windows, the winder handle was forward of the release catch. When the optional electric windows were fitted, a small plug covered the hole for emergency operation with the manual crank. Above the winder position was an anodised black radio speaker grille; this bore the only badge on the car that actually read 'Ferrari GTO', in black on a yellow background. The door pull was to the rear of the speaker and contained an interior light on the forward face.

Driver and passenger sun visors were provided, that on the passenger's side containing a vanity mirror. Between the sun visors was the dipping interior mirror, secured to the windscreen by an adhesive pad.

Dashboard & Instruments

The main instrument panel, finished in matt black and contained in a deep hooded nacelle, was of a similar shape to that of contemporary 308/328 models. Like other Ferraris of the time, all of the Veglia-manufactured dials were black-faced with markings and needles in orange.

On the left of the panel was the 320kph speedometer (an mph unit was not offered), incorporating distance recorder, trip meter and warning lights for parking lights and direction indicators. In the centre were two gauges for turbo boost pressure (upper, with an excessive pressure warning light) and oil pressure (lower, with a low pressure warning light). On the right was the 10,000rpm rev counter, which had the red line marked at 7800rpm and incorporated warning lights for high beam, rear fog lights and handbrake/brake failure.

A few other items were gathered on the instrument panel. To the lower left of the speedometer was an indicator light for the hazard warning lights, while in a matching position at lower right was the trip meter reset control. Either side of the small dials were lights to indicate that the left or right ventilation fans were in operation. To the bottom left of the rev counter was the ignition/generator warning light.

A sub-panel in the centre of the dashboard contained a row of three gauges, angled towards the driver. From the left, these covered water temperature, oil temperature and fuel. Below the gauges were twin, rectangular, adjustable ventilation outlets, with left-hand and right-hand air conditioning temperature controls either side when this option was fitted.

The dash top had a windscreen demister slot at each extremity, with three circular multi-direction outlets in the centre section. There was a small oddments opening in the dash face between the steering column and driver's door, with an instrument light rheostat sited nearby. To the right of the column was the ignition switch, with a separate starter button – an appealing traditional touch – to its left.

The Momo steering wheel had a leather rim, three spokes in black anodised aluminium, and a central horn push carrying the obligatory *Cavallino Rampante* on a yellow background. Two left-hand column stalks controlled lights and direction indicators, while a single stalk on the right looked after windscreen wipers (two speeds plus intermittent) and washers.

The rest of the controls were placed between the seats on a raised console, which had an ashtray mounted in the front face. The traditional aluminium open-gate gearchange was at the front on the driver's side, the lever having a chrome-plated shaft topped with a black plastic ball inscribed with the gearchange pattern in white. Alongside the gearchange gate, on the right of the console, were levers for left and right cabin temperature control, with behind them a matching pair for left and right air distribution. On the driver's side the panel then sloped down towards the rear and contained a cigarette lighter, plus electric window switches (where fitted), while a chrome

With orange-on-black dials, 320kph speedometer and 7800rpm-lined rev counter dominate main instrument panel. Dashboard centre panel contains gauges for water temperature, oil temperature and fuel, below which are fan and temperature control knobs either side of directional ventilation outlets.

Front compartment houses spacesaver spare wheel under zipped cover and water radiator with twin electric fans. There was no dedicated luggage space in the GTO…

Cavallino Rampante was placed on the horizontal face. The passenger's side of the console sloped down from the rear of the heater controls, and contained a bank of four switches for left and right ventilation fans, hazard warning lights and rear fog lights (where fitted). The handbrake was at the rear of the console.

The fuse/relay board was fitted behind a panel under the passenger's side of the dashboard. The pull for releasing the oil filler flap was on the upper rear bulkhead to the right of the passenger seat.

Luggage Compartment

In the 288 GTO you had to travel light as there was no real luggage compartment. Small items could be wedged in behind the seats if they were not at their rearmost position, otherwise it was a case of arranging small, soft bags around the spacesaver spare wheel in the front compartment. If additional space was required, the only alternative was to leave the spare wheel or passenger at home!

The front compartment also contained, in a separate forward section, the front-mounted radiator with twin thermostatically controlled cooling fans. The left-hand lower front was occupied by twin air horns with their compressor forward of the wheel arch, while the other front corner contained the left and right cockpit ventilation fans, which were linked to the heater boxes and air outlet points by flexible tubes. When air conditioning was fitted, the condenser coil with cooling fan was sited in the left-hand front wheel arch, behind the air horns; the air conditioning compressor was belt-driven off the engine and mounted to the lower right of it. The air conditioning unit served the three circular dashboard outlets and the pair of rectangular directional vents on the centre dash console.

The battery was housed in a separate compartment below the spare wheel. The contents of the tool kit, stowed in two soft bags around the spare wheel, are listed in the panel. At upper left on the bulkhead were the brake master cylinder, servo unit and combined brake/clutch fluid reservoir, while the windscreen washer reservoir was on the right.

Tool Kit

Bag 1
- Set of 6-22mm open-end spanners
- Long pliers, 180mm
- Flat-blade screwdriver, 120mm long
- Flat-blade screwdriver, 150mm long
- Phillips screwdriver, 4mm diameter
- Phillips screwdriver, 5-9mm diameter

Bag 2
- Scissor jack
- Jack ratchet handle
- Emergency triangle
- Lead mallet
- Wheel nut wrench
- Spark plug spanner
- Alternator belt
- Air conditioner compressor belt (where fitted)
- Water pump belt
- Towing eye-bolt
- Spare bulbs
- Sparking plugs (2)

Engine

The 288 GTO was Ferrari's first mid-engined V8 production car with a longitudinal engine. The engine, clutch, differential and gearbox were mounted in line, with the gearbox end case and its cast Ferrari script badge visible under the rear valance of the car. The all-alloy type F114B engine of 2855cc (174.2cu in), with bore and stroke of 80mm (3.15in) by 71mm (2.79in), was equipped with twin turbochargers and produced claimed maximum power of 400bhp at 7000rpm and maximum torque of 366lb ft (50.6kgm) at 3800rpm.

The engine layout was Ferrari's standard 90° vee configuration, with twin overhead camshafts per bank of cylinders, each bank having its own toothed drive belt and tensioner assembly, driven off pulleys that were connected to transfer gears driven off a gear wheel keyed to the crankshaft. There were four valves per cylinder, the two camshafts on each bank respectively actuating paired inlet and exhaust valves through bucket tappets and spacer shims. Each bank of cylinders had its own distributor driven off the end of the inlet camshaft. On each head the twin inlet and exhaust valves were inclined at an angle of 46° with respect to each other; timing data is given below.

Timing Data

Inlets open BTDC	16°
Inlets close ABDC	48°
Exhausts open BBDC	54°
Exhausts close ATDC	10°

Valve timing should be measured with a clearance of 0.50mm between the tappet thimbles and camshaft. Valve clearances with cold engine should be 0.20-0.25mm for inlet valves and 0.35-0.40mm for exhaust valves, measured between the valve pads and camshaft. Firing order is 1-5-3-7-4-8-2-6.

The pistons were flat-topped with a recessed crown and a twin-plus-oil-control ring assembly. White metal bearings were used on the lightweight, balanced connecting rods, of ring type on the small end and split shell on the big end. The forged steel crankshaft, machined from a solid billet, featured five main bearings, and at its nose were a camshaft drive gear, an oil pump drive chain wheel and a bolted-on main pulley. The flywheel was bolted to the rear end of the crankshaft.

Dry-sump lubrication was employed, utilising a high-pressure, twin-circuit pump mounted within the beautiful, ribbed magnesium alloy sump. The

Twin-turbocharged 2855cc, 400bhp engine with red intake castings nestles under cabin firewall, twin Behr intercoolers – with turbo wastegate between – dominating space behind. Access to forward part of engine is through removable section of firewall.

SYSTEM CAPACITIES (LITRES)

Fuel tank	120
Cooling system	17
Washer bottle	2.5
Engine oil	12.5
Gearbox oil	5

After-market option twin megaphone exhaust system produces deep burble at tickover, and shrill, F1-like sound at high revs. Gearbox end cover protrudes below rear valance, and proudly proclaims its heritage.

pump was directly chain-driven off the crankshaft immediately above it, and had two screened pick-up points at either end of the sump, pushing the oil via the filter to a cooler radiator in the engine bay, then back to the oil tank on the right of the engine bay. The second circuit pulled oil from the tank and blew it through eight spray nozzles onto the underside of the piston crowns to aid cooling. The cap of the oil tank incorporated a dipstick to check capacity level. The engine oil filter was mounted at an angle in the centre of the vee at the rear of the engine.

The water pump was driven by a grooved belt from the main crankshaft pulley, and was sited in the engine vee at the front end, with a belt tensioner assembly between, and to the right of, the pump and main pulleys. The cooling system header tank was mounted on the left of the engine bay.

The alternator was mounted to the lower left front side of the engine, and belt-driven off the main crankshaft pulley with its own tensioner. The air conditioning compressor, when fitted, occupied a similar location on the right, while the starter motor was on the left of the engine, bolted to the flywheel casing.

The combined ignition/injection system was a Weber-Marelli IAW unit for each bank of cylinders. Each comprised a microprocessor electronic control unit, inlet air pressure sensor, ignition coil, additional air valve, throttle potentiometer, fuel injectors, water temperature sensor, distributor, engine speed pick-ups and air temperature sensor – all of these combined to provide the right fuel/air mixture to the engine under all conditions.

The air supply to this system was introduced by a twin turbocharger installation, exhaust-driven, with an IHI turbocharger for each bank of cylinders. Air was provided through a Behr intercooler to reduce the inlet air temperature. The intake air was initially introduced via an air box with filter for each bank of cylinders, mounted at the rear of the engine bay and drawing air through the engine cover louvres.

Fuel storage was in two aluminium tanks, one on each side of the forward end of the engine bay, with a balance pipe between them. Each tank served the injection system for one bank of cylinders via an electric in-line pump and fuel filter.

The exhaust system provided to each bank of cylinders a pair of free-flow tubular manifolds (with a sheet steel shroud) to feed the appropriate turbocharger. Exhaust gas analysis tappings were provided on each pipe, between the manifold and turbocharger. From each turbocharger the exhaust pipe fed into a single horizontal silencer box, mounted across the inside of the tail panel. This had a central connection that led to a common wastegate, which fed back to the exhaust pipes on the turbocharger inlets, to reduce turbo lag. The exhaust gases finally exited via a pipe on each side of the silencer box, dropping vertically, then turning rearward into twin chrome tailpipes exiting through cut-outs in the lower edge of the valance. A twin megaphone sports exhaust system, one per bank, was available as an after-market option.

TRANSMISSION

The all-synchromesh five-speed gearbox was mounted on the rear of the differential casing, which in turn was mounted on the clutch housing that bolted to the main engine block. All the transmission housings were cast from lightweight magnesium/aluminium alloy, and heavily ribbed externally to provide additional strength and cooling.

The clutch was an 8.5in diameter dry twin-plate unit with a diaphragm pressure plate, mounted on the

OVERALL GEAR RATIOS

First	1:10.707
Second	1:6.659
Third	1:4.745
Fourth	1:3.723
Fifth	1:2.964
Reverse	1:9.518
Final drive	10/29

flywheel and hydraulically operated via a master cylinder in the pedal box and a slave cylinder built into the clutch housing. Power was transmitted through the clutch shaft to a drop gear mounted on the rear end of it; this meshed with another on the gearbox main shaft, which passed under the differential into the gearbox.

The gearbox oil pump was driven directly off the end of the main shaft, its casing being cast into the gearbox end cover; there was a tubular gauze filter on the pump inlet. The gears were arranged on the main shaft in the order, from the front, of first, reverse, third, second, fifth and fourth. Directly above the main shaft was the lay shaft, upon which were mounted the secondary gears and synchroniser rings, with the crown wheel pinion on its front end. Reverse gear had an intermediate idler gear to reverse the direction of motion. All shafts ran in roller bearings.

The differential crown wheel fed off the spur gear on the end of the gearbox lay shaft. It was housed in an aluminium casing that was bolted at the rear to the gearbox, with which it shared lubrication oil, and at the front to the clutch housing. Flanged drive shaft couplings exited the casing on either side and ran in roller bearings, with the drive shafts featuring universal joints encased in rubber boots at both ends.

Gear selection was via three selector forks – one each for first and reverse, second and third, and fourth and fifth – actuated by solid rods running within the left-hand side of the gearbox, with the main control shaft and lever in the bottom left of the 'box, where the shaft from the gear lever entered the casing. This linkage had a pair of universal joints along its length, together with a threaded adjuster at its rear end.

The speedometer was actuated by an electronic pulse unit mounted in the gearbox rear end plate.

ELECTRICAL EQUIPMENT & LIGHTS

The electrical system was a 12-volt, negative earth system, served by a 66Ah battery fed by a Bosch 65A alternator.

Lighting equipment was the same on all GTOs, except that those for French customers were fitted with yellow lenses to comply with legislation at that time. The headlights were single 7in diameter units housed in retractable pods in the front wings. The pod motors were actuated by relays fed from the light switch, raising them when the lights were switched on. The motors were fitted with a knurled knob to effect manual operation in case of failure. Headlight bulbs were 55/60 watt high/low beam halogen H4 iodine vapour type.

The front sidelights/indicators were slim, rectangular units in the bumper extremities, with white and amber lenses respectively. Below the bumper, on each side of the radiator grille, were a pair of rectangular driving lights, with 55 watt halogen bulbs. The inner was a supplementary high beam and daytime flasher, while the outer unit operated only as a daytime flasher. Small, circular, amber direction indicator repeaters were fitted on the front wings just forward of the wheel arch.

The rear light assemblies were Ferrari's traditional twin circular units on each side of the tail panel. The outer units were amber for direction indicators, with a circular white reversing light in the centre. The inner units were red with rear and brake lights in the outer ring and a circular reflector in the centre. The number plate lights were mounted on the inner ends of the quarter bumpers, housed in circular chrome cases. Rear fog warning lights were available as an extra, and when fitted were mounted on brackets that suspended them below the quarter bumpers at the outer end.

MAJOR ELECTRICAL EQUIPMENT

Battery	12V 66Ah
Alternator	Bosch 65A
Starter motor	Bosch 0.001.110.004
Injection/ignition	Weber-Marelli IAW
Sparking plugs	Champion A596G (12mm)

SUSPENSION & STEERING

Suspension was independent all round, with unequal-length wishbones in welded high-tensile tubular steel, coil springs and double-acting shock absorbers.

The Koni shock absorbers, of types 82 P 2279 (front) and 82 P 2073 (rear), were mounted within the coil springs. At the front these spring/shock absorber assemblies were fitted between the wishbone arms, but at the rear they were located between the top of the upper wishbone and the chassis suspension turret, because the drive shafts passed between the wishbones. Front and rear anti-roll bars linked the suspension units on each side of the car. The hub carrier assemblies were very similar in layout to those used on all V8 models since the 308 GT4, but they were constructed from aluminium; bearings and mountings also followed the practice established on the earlier models.

Steering was by rack and pinion, with a collapsible

SUSPENSION SETTINGS

Front toe-in	1.0-2.0mm
Front camber	–0°15′ to –0°30′
Rear toe-in	3.0-4.0mm
Rear camber	–1° to –1°20′

Fixed castor angle should be 5°10′. All settings are applicable to a car in static laden condition: full tank of petrol, two persons on board, 20kg of luggage.

column, and provided a turning circle of 12m (39ft), with 2.89 turns lock to lock. The steering ball joints were sealed for life, and the steering box had an automatic slack take-up facility.

BRAKES

Ventilated disc brakes were provided all round, of 306mm (12.05in) diameter at the front and 310mm (12.20in) at the rear. Each has a twin-pot aluminium alloy caliper fitted with Galfer 1725 FF pads.

Magnificent highly polished split-rim Speedline wheels are unique to GTO.

The hydraulic system was twin-circuit (one each for front and rear) and servo-assisted, and incorporated a rear circuit pressure regulator with a tandem master cylinder, a booster unit and a combined brake/clutch fluid reservoir sited under the front lid. A combined low system pressure/handbrake warning light was provided in the rev counter.

The handbrake was twin cable-operated (one per side) on conventional shoes that acted on the inner surface of the rear disc brake hubs. Manual adjustment was provided on each handbrake cable at the rear, where they passed through a chassis member before separating to their respective wheels.

WHEELS & TYRES

The 288 GTO had wheels manufactured by Speedline that were unique to the model. These had a natural polished and lacquered aluminium split rim, secured to the central part of the wheel with 20 studs, with five silver-painted and lacquered spokes featuring raised ribs on their edges. The central hub spline was retained by a single chrome-plated hub nut bearing the *Cavallino Rampante*. The hub nut seated on a circular chromed steel bearing plate on the centre face of the wheel.

An aluminium spacesaver spare wheel was fitted with a high-pressure tyre, and mounted in a well in the front compartment. All wheel and tyre specifications are listed below.

WHEELS/TYRES

Front wheels	8Jx16
Front tyres	Goodyear NCT 225/50 VR16
Rear wheels	10Jx16
Rear tyres	Goodyear NCT 255/50 VR16
Spacesaver wheel	3.25x19
Spacesaver tyre	Goodyear T105/80 R19

IDENTIFICATION PLATES

The 288 GTO had a standard set of identification plates and labels as follows:

1 Engine type and serial number plate at the front centre of the engine block vee.
2 Vehicle type and chassis number on upper face of right rear suspension turret.
3 Ferrari homologation plate on inner face of right rear suspension turret.
4 Engine and gearbox oil lubrication label on the top face of right-hand air intake box, at rear of engine bay.
5 Anti-freeze label on the side of the radiator header tank on the left of the engine bay.
6 Paint label on inner right face of front lid.
7 Recommended tyre pressure label in corner of wind screen on driver's side.
8 Car type and chassis number plate in an upstand on the upper surface of steering column.
9 Spacesaver spare wheel and tyre labels on wheel and tyre, giving use warnings and recommended tyre operating pressure.

Vehicle Identification Number is located on steering column shroud and right-hand rear suspension upright.

PRODUCTION DATA

Production period	Chassis number range	Number built
1984-86	52465-58345	272

F40 (1987-92)

Low angle of European F40 accentuates purposeful lines of this ultimate 1980s supercar. Adapting words of Henry Ford, you could have any colour you liked as long as it was red…

The F40 was the second of Ferrari's 'Racers For The Road' of the 1980s, and the last new model presented by Enzo Ferrari, at a ceremony in Maranello in June 1987, prior to his death in August 1988. The model took its name from F for Ferrari and 40 for the 40th anniversary of Ferrari car production. This successor to the 288 GTO was even faster and even more radical in appearance, and rather more stark in interior appointments.

Prior to the F40's public announcement, spy photographs of what was thought to be the GTO's successor appeared in motoring magazines worldwide. It later transpired that the stumpy, multi-slotted, multi-winged prototype, which became known as the 288 Evoluzione, was in fact a test bed for the forthcoming F40. Five of these prototypes were built, one of which has been retained by the factory with the others in private collections.

The lineage to the other two-seater V8 models in the range, the 328 GTB/S series, at the time of the F40's announcement was far more remote than that from the GTO to its 308 QV contemporaries. The only trace of its heritage was in the cabin section profile – complete with identical windscreen – and the black-painted indent line in the body sides.

Great care had been taken by Pininfarina in perfecting the aerodynamic profile, resulting in a wide, low, aggressive front that flowed through the cabin section to an even wider rear, dominated by a high-mounted integral wing. If ever a car's appearance was a statement of its intent, then the F40 was it – this was definitely no Q car! From every angle the lines shouted 'power'. This was the fastest production car of the time and it knew it – even the front grille seemed to wear a smirk.

While retaining its Ferrari roots with a tubular steel chassis, the F40 also marked another step forward in the use of composite materials for the lightweight construction of numerous chassis stiffening panels and all bodywork sections.

Unsurprisingly, public and press acclaim for the F40 was universal, and once again queues formed at the factory gates. With customers desperate to get their hands on one, the price spiral accelerated even faster than the car itself.

As with the GTO, all production was in left-hand drive form only, although this time a US market version was produced, so that customers there had no personal import or 'federalisation' problems to contend with. Again the F40 was a limited production model, although after the GTO phenomenon, where new cars had changed hands at well above list price, Ferrari refused to state exactly how many would be produced and over what period.

Open and shut case! Profile shots (facing page) show how entire front and rear body sections open to provide access not only to front compartment and engine bay, but also to suspension/wheel assemblies. Massive rear engine cover is supported by a folding strut, and can be detached by removing roof hinge pins.

Early production models – believed to be the first 50 – had Plexiglas sliding windows, as on this example (above), UK concessionaire's original demonstrator. Later European model (left) with glass winding windows is seen at Ferrari factory; rear fog warning lights in lower tail panel extremities are Europe-only feature, although sometimes they were mounted vertically on grille between rear lights and number plate.

US-spec F40 differed from European version in various details. In front view, deeper front lip spoiler is more prominent, and indent line above grille opening is filled with a rubber strip that runs round to slim side marker lights. At rear, black rubber strip is repeated (and thicker), side marker light is surface-mounted between wheel arch and wing slots, no rear fog warning lights are fitted, and mandatory high-level brake light is just visible on engine cover, above Ferrari badge.

High-level views of 288 Evoluzione amply illustrate how F40 shape evolved from this early test bed for composite structures and turbocharged GTO engine development. It was only necessary to lengthen nose and tail panels slightly, and integrate rear wing, to achieve definitive F40 shape.

At the instigation of the French importer, Pozzi Ferrari France, a racing version was developed in conjunction with Michelotto of Padova (Padua). Known as the F40LM, this was raced with some success in the IMSA category in the US in 1989/90. Subsequently more examples of the F40LM were built for racing customers, and some road cars were converted to this specification for track use.

With the resurgence of GT and sports car racing in the 1990s, further development took place and Ferrari Club Italia campaigned two cars designated F40GT-Es during 1995, in the BPR endurance race series. These same two cars were again successfully campaigned during 1996 by the Ennea-Igol team, which occasionally fielded a third car. Concurrently, a French-entered car modified from a standard F40 to F40LM specification contested the series, with occasional appearances by other examples in varying degrees of modification. Nine years after introduction, and four years after the end of production, race-prepared F40s were still proving to be competitive at the top level of GT car racing, while still turning heads whenever seen on the road.

Body & Chassis

As with the 288 GTO that preceded it, the F40 had a separate tubular steel chassis. This differed very little in overall concept, with oval main tubes plus square and rectangular tubular sub-assemblies, but it was supplemented by substantial use of composites to add strength, notably for deep sill box sections, sill exten-

Four views of non-production F40 relatives: multi-slot rear of 288 Evoluzione (top left); pre-production F40 prototype (centre left) with five slots in rear wing – instead of four – and different vent pattern in Plexiglas engine cover; F40 LM (bottom left) competition derivative of 1989-90, with large radiator air outlet in front lid, fixed headlights under cowls, front lip spoiler, larger diameter wheels and adjustable rear wing; racing F40 GT-E (below) of 1995-96, developed from F40 LM and very quick in 'old age', seen in Ennea-Igol livery as campaigned during 1996.

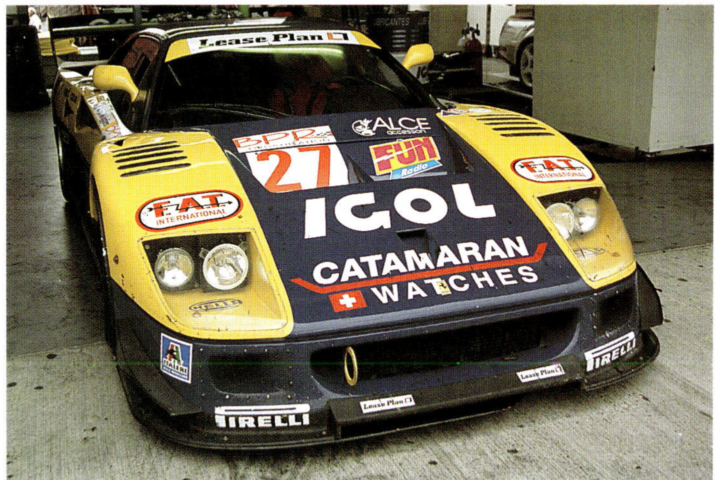

sions up the inner door posts to the glass line, the cabin floor pan, dashboard and front bulkhead. These composite panels, like the roof, were bonded to the chassis using a specially formulated 'structural adhesive' with a green appearance.

The rear bulkhead featured additional circular tubing, extending through the horizontal top face of it in front of the rear screen and connecting to the roll hoop above the screen, to make an even more rigid chassis frame. These tubes were visible on the inside and through the rear window. As the F40 had fully-opening rear bodywork, easily removable by extracting the roof hinge pins, the rear section of the chassis was formed from continuous tubes, abandoning the square-flanged detachable mountings provided for the rear chassis section of the GTO.

Wide horizontal sill sections sat proud of the doors, and small outriggers were welded to the main chassis tubes to support these. Due to stricter worldwide crash test legislation, the front chassis tube arrangement provided a progressively deformable structure. The engine/cabin firewall was an aluminium and composite honeycomb three-piece panel with a removable centre section for access to the front of the engine. A composite undertray was attached to the underside of the chassis by pop rivets, and extended from the front axle line to the back of the cabin section.

The F40's bodywork consisted of only 11 main panels: a one-piece front end, a roof section, a pair of doors, a pair of sills, a pair of rear quarter wings, a one-piece tail section, a rear aerofoil and a rear valance. All of these were manufactured from a composite weave of Nomex, Kevlar and carbon-fibre, which combined great strength with light weight. The F40 was the first road car to utilise these materials to such a large degree, previous automotive use having been limited to small elements, as on the GTO.

The one-piece front panel hinged at the lower forward edge, and was retained by catches on the slim section between the wheel arch and door line. The front radiator intake opening was flanked by large brake cooling inlet ducts, with a small black rubber spoiler attached to the lower edge of the nose. On US models this spoiler section was a much more pronounced appendage, which rather destroyed the elegant yet aggressive frontal appearance. In addition to this, US cars featured projecting black rubber inserts in the indent line at the front and rear of the car, again compromising the fluidity of line.

The front lid also included two small NACA ducts on its upper face to feed the interior ventilation system. The trailing edge of the front wing sections protruded out from the door profile, creating a slender duct faced with black plastic louvres for the exit of brake cooling air; radiator air was expelled under the car. A towing eye contained in the tool kit could be screwed into a socket on the right-hand side of the nose, after removing a body-coloured insert.

The Pininfarina/Ferrari black indent line along the body sides was a familiar feature, but on the F40 it also continued around the front and rear perimeters. The doors contained long, slim, triangulated intake slots that continued into the rear wing quarter panels and provided engine bay cooling air. On each lower rear wing quarter panel a NACA duct fed cooling air to the rear brakes. The rear buttresses contained intake scoops from the trailing edge of the curved quarter window glass, these being ducted to the air filter box for each bank of cylinders.

The rear lid, with its prominent wing, had slots and openings almost everywhere. Alongside the buttresses were two NACA ducts to feed air to the gearbox oil cooler (left) and the engine oil cooler (right). Behind these, surrounding the screen, were a series of slots to extract hot air, and there were a further 11 horizontal slots in the Plexiglas curved rear screen – which gave a splendid view of the engine bay – and four vertical slots on each rear wing side, between the wheel arch and the tail. Prototype models, incidentally, had a larger number of smaller slots in the rear screen and five vertical rear wing slots per side.

The inset rear face of the tail panel was a matt black diamond mesh with paired apertures for the light units at each end. Rectangular catches were provided at each side of the tail panel and were secured to the rear valance panel. This valance had an oval opening for the exhaust pipes in the centre, a venturi hollow to either side, and deep extremities with slotted sections beneath to extract hot air from the engine and gearbox oil coolers. When opened, the tail panel was supported by a folding rod that extended from the inner valance.

The F40 was never homologated by the factory for the Swiss market, so customers there had to register their cars outside Switzerland, or drive on trade plates, or effect modifications to obtain homologation for road use. One of the main obstacles was the height of the rear wing above the body, which in Switzerland must not exceed 80mm (3.15in). In some instances the support stanchions were lowered to meet the requirements, while Symbol Automobiles SA came up with the solution of an infill section, effectively raising the rear body upper surface towards the standard wing to satisfy legislation.

DIMENSIONS & WEIGHTS

Overall length (EU)	4358mm (171.6in)
Overall length (US)	4400mm (173.2in)
Overall width	1970mm (77.6in)
Overall height	1124mm (44.3in)
Wheelbase	2450mm (96.5in)
Front track	1594mm (62.8in)
Rear track	1606mm (63.2in)
Dry weight (EU)	1235kg (2723lb)
Dry weight (US)	1350kg (2976lb)

OPTIONAL EQUIPMENT

Adjustable suspension
Fitted luggage

Air intakes abound, as shown in these detail shots: along door/rear wing, supplying intercoolers (upper left); behind rear quarter windows, supplying turbochargers (upper right); one of the pair of front lid NACA ducts, supplying air conditioning system (lower left); NACA duct on lower rear wing, supplying rear brakes (lower right).

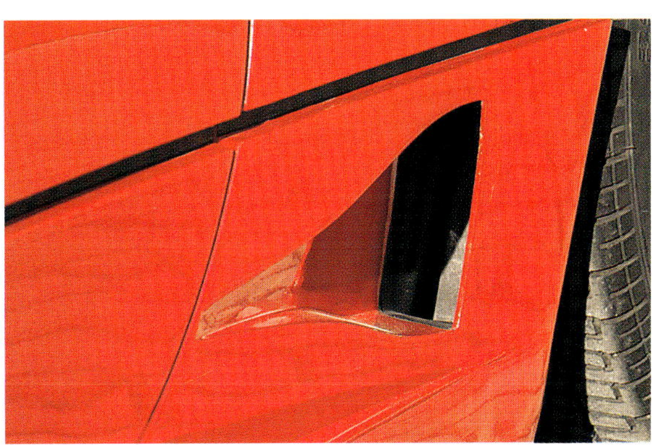

Elegantly machined fuel filler cap (below), with Kevlar construction of cover flap clearly visible on its inside face. Radiator air outlets (below right) are incorporated in trailing edges of protruding front wings.

Body Trim & Fittings

In keeping with its statement of purpose, the body had very little adornment. The door and side window frames were black anodised aluminium, while the glued-in windscreen – a component shared with the 308/328 GTB/S series – and inner cabin rear screen had black rubber surrounds.

A large, single windscreen wiper was provided, with a twin jet washer system for the two sides of its arc. The wiper arm and blade were hidden in the parked position by the rear edge of the front lid. The windscreen was tinted, with a more heavily tinted band across the top. Where glass winding windows were fitted in the doors, these were also tinted. The prototypes and – according to the general consensus of opinion – the first 50 production cars had impractical Plexiglas door windows with a small sliding panel in the shape of a parallelogram.

The prototypes also had their door mirrors mounted on arms that protruded from the front corner of the door glass area, but for production cars there were revised mirrors – a change necessary to satisfy regulations concerning their field of view –

mounted on angled, body colour arms fixed to the top face of the door panel.

The top face of each rear quarter wing section contained an oval fuel filler flap made of composite, each of the two Ferrari-badged filler caps being most elegantly crafted in aluminium. The front and rear lids were secured by rectangular matt black levers, in the positions previously noted, that featured chromed lock barrels. The door handles were small, flush, body colour pull levers in the upper rear face of the doors, and again the lock barrels were chromed.

The front lid featured the traditional enamel Ferrari badge at the front, with recessed enamel Scuderia Ferrari shields mounted on the front wing sides above the release catches. Rectangular 'Disegno di Pininfarina' aluminium badges were fitted on the rear wing quarter panels above the black indent line; on prototypes the location of these badges varied or they were missing completely. A recessed F40 logo was moulded into the outer face of the right-hand rear wing support, but again some prototypes lacked this feature. The tail panel featured an aluminium Ferrari script badge, mounted centrally on the thin body strip above the inset mesh.

PAINTWORK

As with the GTO, customers had a single colour choice, Rosso Corsa FER 300/9, any other colour being a post-factory alteration. Apart from the matt black body indent line, window surrounds and grilles, all other elements of the external bodywork were red.

INTERIOR TRIM & FITTINGS

One word sums up this section – sparse! Customer choice was also even more limited than on the GTO.

The bucket seats, of simple one-piece design although elaborate to manufacture, each comprised a Kevlar shell faced with red cloth. Having the squab and backrest integral meant that there could be no rake adjustment, so only the fore/aft position could be altered, by a bar under the front edge. Three-point inertia reel seat belts were standard, each seat moulding having three apertures to accommodate both belt and catch.

There was virtually no interior trim, most of the surfaces remaining bare or painted composite material. The roof lining was white perforated plastic similar to that in the GTO, while the dashboard and central tunnel had a black felt-like covering. The floors, sills, footwells, door cavities and seat backs were completely bare, although their exposed composite weave lent a certain decorative appeal. This minimal approach added to the F40's charisma as a 'racing car for the road', but meant that noise levels in the cabin, which acted like a sounding box, were very high.

The steering wheel rim was trimmed with black

Three identifying details: moulded F40 logo on right-hand rear aerofoil upright; enamel Scuderia Ferrari shields on front wings; Ferrari script on engine cover, with US high-level brake light visible above.

One reason for F40's technical fascination: close-up of composite weave in Nomex, Kevlar and carbon-fibre, seen in sill area; bright green line is 'structural adhesive'.

No-frills cockpit for serious drivers contains one-piece Kevlar seat shells faced with bright red cloth; lateral support is superb, much better than in 288 GTO. Notable features include high sills and central tunnel carrying only gearchange and handbrake; door appearance varies with winding glass windows (above) and sliding Plexiglas windows (right).

suede, the three spokes were black anodised aluminium (with the manufacturer's Momo logo in yellow on the lower spoke), and the centre section – containing six Allen bolts to secure the wheel to the column – featured a yellow horn push with black *Cavallino Rampante*.

Large openings in the door shells provided generous storage room. Across the centre of each opening was a black plastic-covered cable for door release. A manual window winder was provided on the door face just ahead of the open section on cars with glass door windows. Early F40s with Plexiglas windows had a small sliding panel secured by a crude Plexiglas catch, which was flimsily attached by three screws to the fixed part of the window.

Driver and passenger sun visors were provided, the one on the passenger side containing a vanity mirror. Between the sun visors was a central dipping interior mirror, fixed to the windscreen by an adhesive pad. The fuse/relay panel was fitted behind a removable panel on the face of the passenger side of the dashboard, the cover being retained by a chromed screw at each corner.

Ferrari's uncompromising quest for lightness with F40: no Wilton carpet, just a rubber heel mat on Kevlar floor and drilled pedals for driver's feet to dance upon.

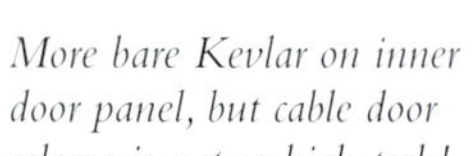

More bare Kevlar on inner door panel, but cable door release is not so high-tech!

DASHBOARD & INSTRUMENTS

As with the GTO, the main instruments were contained in a hooded nacelle in front of the driver, although the layout was different. The Veglia-Borletti instruments all had white markings on black faces.

The two main instruments were the speedometer and rev counter. On the left, the 220mph or 360kph speedometer incorporated the distance recorder, trip meter and warning lights for direction indicators, rear fog lights (where fitted) and main beam. On the right, the 10,000rpm rev counter had an orange sector marked from 7700rpm, and warning lights in the bottom segment for ignition, brake failure/handbrake and height regulation system failure. Between these two main dials were warning lights for low oil pressure (upper) and high water temperature (lower), and two knobs at the bottom for trip meter re-set and instrument light rheostat.

In the bottom corners of the panel were small gauges for water temperature (left) and turbo boost pressure (right), the latter incorporating a warning light for excessive boost. On cars with catalytic converters, a warning light was added above each of these gauges, indicating that the converter was overheating on the appropriate left or right cylinder bank.

A line of three dials in the centre of the dashboard covered, from left, oil temperature, oil pressure and fuel level. Below these were two rotary knobs for the air conditioning – a standard feature! – controlling air volume (left) and temperature (right). Closer to the steering column was the ignition switch, with a separate push button for the starter to its lower left. Five

Driver information is kept deliberately simple. Main instrument panel houses two most important auxiliary dials (water temperature and turbo boost pressure), while three more are sited in dashboard centre section, along with simple vents and controls for standard air conditioning.

TOOL KIT

Bag 1
Puncture repair bottle
Tyre pressure gauge

Bag 2
Sparking plugs (10)
Water pump/alternator belt
Spare bulbs
Wheel nut spanner
Towing eye-bolt
Spare wheel nut pins (4)
Set of 6-22mm open-end spanners
Plain screwdriver, 120mm
Phillips screwdriver, 5-9mm diameter
Universal pliers, 180mm
Sparking plug spanner with ratchet drive

Space for luggage in front compartment was an improvement over the 288 GTO, mainly due to omission of spare wheel; the two tool bags are seen. Enormous front lid has central mouldings to feed air conditioning system from twin NACA ducts into a single aperture, which mates, when lid is closed, against perforated grille below windscreen.

circular, directionally adjustable air outlets were positioned centrally on the dashboard, two on top for windscreen demisting and three below for normal cockpit ventilation.

Tucked away to the left of the steering column was a row of four rectangular switches controlling, from left, ride height (where fitted), windscreen heating, headlight cover defrosting and rear fog lights (where fitted), and to the right of these was a circular push button for the hazard warning lights.

The three column stalks followed the standard Ferrari arrangement: long and short stalks on the left for lights and direction indicators respectively, and one stalk on the right controlling the single wiper blade (two-speed plus intermittent) and washers.

The central tunnel housed the traditional open-gate gearchange, with a chrome lever surmounted by a black plastic ball inscribed in white with the gear positions. To the rear of the gate was a small, recessed oddments tray and the handbrake lever.

Luggage Compartment

Luggage space was an improvement on the GTO as there was no spare wheel, so a reasonably deep well was available, maximised by using the optional fitted luggage made in leather by Schedoni.

Lifting the one-piece nose section reveals the whole front end of the car, with the water radiator and twin thermostatically controlled cooling fans at the very front, and a moulded luggage well behind it. In the base of this well is a removable panel giving access to the battery, which has a rotary master isolating switch on the upper left of the well, just in front of the brake master cylinder and reservoir. On the right-hand side is the windscreen washer reservoir, with two tool bags alongside it. The contents of the tool bags are listed in the panel on the facing page.

Engine

In general configuration the F40's twin-turbocharged engine was virtually identical to that of the 288 GTO, but in the three years that had elapsed since the GTO's introduction a great of development work had taken place with the 288 Evoluzione prototypes, resulting in numerous detail changes to the specification and a significant increase in power.

The F40 engine, type reference F120A, was slightly enlarged at 2936cc (179.16cu in), with the bore increased from 80mm (3.15in) to 81.9mm (3.22in) and the stroke shortened from 71mm (2.79in) to 69.5mm (2.74in). There was also a nominal increase in compression ratio from 7.6:1 to 7.7:1. The factory quoted the power output at 478bhp at 7000rpm, a handsome improvement on the 400bhp of the GTO. Just as significant to performance were the much improved torque characteristics, the peak figure rising from the GTO's 366lb ft (50.6kgm) at 3800rpm to 425lb ft (58.8kgm) at 4000rpm; torque for the US model was given as 424lb ft (58.6kgm) at 4500rpm.

The piston crowns were redesigned to provide a 'squish' effect in the combustion chamber, aiding gas flow with a higher boost pressure, up from 0.8 bar to 1.1 bar maximum. The IHI RHB 53LW turbochargers were water-cooled to aid efficiency and prolong bearing life, while the Behr intercoolers were positioned at an angle to improve air flow through them. The wastegate featured a discharge direct to atmosphere through the silencer central exhaust pipe outlet, and actuation was controlled by the injection control unit of cylinder bank 1-4 via a solenoid valve. The turbocharging control system was set by the factory to optimise its performance against

the particular engine characteristics, thus providing maximum boost to coincide with the torque zone.

The combined injection/ignition system was again the Weber-Marelli IAW unit, with the electronic control master units for each bank now mounted in the cabin on the firewall behind the seats. All other engine ancillaries were mounted in the same positions as on the GTO. Timing data was also shared with the GTO (see page 105).

Petrol storage was in a similar location to the GTO, in twin tanks mounted at either side of the forward end of the engine bay. Whereas the GTO had aluminium tanks, those on the F40 were racing-type rubber fuel cells encased in sponge. A central balance pipe allowed both tanks to be replenished through either filler.

The exhaust manifolds followed the same basic construction and layout as the GTO, except that twin catalytic converters were fitted to all F40s except the earliest European versions. Each manifold collector pipe fed its appropriate turbocharger, before passing gases through the catalytic converter to the silencer box across the tail of the car, and from there to twin, chromed, oval-section tail-pipes, exiting either side of the circular wastegate exhaust through an opening in the centre of the rear valance panel.

To comply with tougher emissions regulations, US models also featured an air injection system to the exhaust manifolds, an evaporative emission control system to prevent petrol vapour escaping from the intake systems, a separate charcoal canister, and a fluid/vapour separating manifold (with electronic control valve) for each bank of cylinders.

European models without catalytic converters needed four-star premium fuel, while those with catalytic converters ran on unleaded fuel. Strangely, the factory quoted identical power output figures for both European and US versions, although performance figures are notably slower for the US model.

TRANSMISSION

The complete gearbox/clutch/final drive assembly was of exactly the same layout as the 288 GTO, as was its method of operation, but the ratios – listed in the panel on page 124 – altered slightly. The only differences were the option of a 'sports' gearbox – a non-synchromesh 'box with dog clutches – and the

Truly a racing car for the road. Note three-outlet exhaust (central pipe serves turbo wastegate), separate radiators each side of tail for engine and gearbox oil, and massive 335/35 tyres – Pirelli P Zero in this instance – with asymmetric tread. All aluminium castings should have a natural finish, as seen on the US-spec car on the facing page.

SYSTEM CAPACITIES (LITRES)

Fuel tank	120
Cooling system	17
Washer bottle	3
Engine oil	10
Gearbox oil	5

Front lighting arrangement, with direction indicator and daytime flasher under a clear shield containing heating elements to prevent misting up, retractable main/dipped beam headlight unit above.

Overall Gear Ratios

	Europe	US
First	1:10.069	1:10.707
Second	1:6.262	1:6.628
Third	1:4.463	1:4.745
Fourth	1:3.501	1:3.724
Fifth	1:2.787	1:2.965
Reverse	1:8.951	1:9.220
Final drive	11/30	10/29

provision of a gearbox oil cooler, mounted in the right-hand side of the rear valance panel, with flexible hose connections to the gearbox.

Electrical Equipment & Lights

The electrical system was 12-volt negative earth, served by a 60Ah battery which was fed by a Bosch 105A alternator.

Lighting conformed to most world requirements, needing only relatively minor changes for certain markets – such as headlight lens colour and dipping arrangement – plus the addition of side marker lights and the omission of rear fog warning lights for cars sold in the US.

Like all other V8-powered Ferraris, the F40's rectangular homofocal headlights – with outer sections for dipped beam and inner sections for main beam – were housed in electrically raised pods on the front wing portions of the one-piece nose panel, and there was the usual manual emergency operation facility. Immediately below each pod, a glass panel with demisting elements protected a recessed light cluster in a matt black surround panel, containing a combined sidelight/indicator on the outside and a high-intensity daytime flasher light next to it.

European models had a small, circular, amber indicator repeater on the side of each front wing, just forward of the wheel arch. US versions differed in having a slim, rectangular unit in a lower position, set into the body indent line. The red side marker lights on the rear wings of US versions were surface-mounted above the indent line, between the wing louvres and wheel arch.

The rear lights were paired circular units mounted in apertures through the recessed tail mesh panel. The outer unit was the amber direction indicator, with a circular white reversing light in the centre. Inboard of this was the red side/brake light with a circular central reflector section. A pair of small rectangular number plate lights were mounted in the centre top edge of the recess. On European models rectangular fog warning lights were normally flush-mounted in cut-outs in the outer faces of the rear valance panel, although some early examples had these lights mounted vertically in the black rear grille, inboard of the other light units.

Major Electrical Equipment

Battery	12V 60Ah
Alternator	Bosch 105A
Starter motor	Bosch
Injection/ignition	Weber-Marelli IAW
Sparking plugs	Champion G61 (10mm)

Suspension & Steering

The basic layout of all-independent wishbone suspension followed on from all the preceding models. Factory press information on the F40's launch spoke of adjustable ride height – with three levels for 'manoeuvring', 'normal' and 'sport' – from the introduction of the model, but this system was not initially available and remained an option when it finally appeared.

Rack and pinion steering was unchanged from the GTO, except that the same 2.89 turns lock to lock gave a slightly reduced turning circle of 11.6m (38ft).

When adjustable suspension was fitted, the ride height setting of the hydraulic shock absorbers could be altered electronically by a switch on the dashboard. This actuated the system's intelligent Electronic Control Unit (ECU), which monitored speed relative to setting and altered the ride height if the speed was not in the appropriate range. The maximum ride height of 150mm (5.9in) for manoeuvring could only be used up to 50kph (31mph), at which point the suspension automatically switched to the medium

Suspension Settings

Front toe-in	1.5-2.5mm
Front camber	−1°10′ to −1°30′
Rear toe-in	2.5-3.5mm
Rear camber	−1° to −1°20′

Fixed castor angle should be between 5°10′ and 5°20′. All settings are applicable to a car in static laden condition: full tank of petrol, two persons on board, 20kg of luggage.

height of 125mm (4.9in) up to 90kph (56mph), and then to the minimum height of 105mm (4.1in) above this speed. The ECU and electro-hydraulic control unit were fitted in the front compartment.

On cars with normal suspension the double-acting Koni shock absorbers were of types 82-8322 (front) and 82-8325 (rear), each mounted within the coil spring, between the wishbones at the front and above the upper wishbone at the rear. The hub carriers were cast aluminium to reduce unsprung weight, but were otherwise very similar in concept to those provided on all the mid-engined V8 cars. Suspension settings differed from those of the GTO and are itemised in the panel on the facing page.

Brakes

The brakes, developed in conjunction with Brembo, were rather more sophisticated than those of the GTO. Ventilated and cross-drilled discs of 332mm (13.1in) diameter were provided all round, and, in order to reduce unsprung weight, they were of composite construction with a cast iron disc mounted on an aluminium hub or 'bell'.

The large aluminium calipers contained four pistons to actuate the Pagid RS4-2 pads, and featured an automatic pad wear take-up mechanism. The handbrake had its own small caliper to each rear disc, fitted opposite the main caliper and mechanically operated from the handbrake lever; the handbrake pads were Ferrari part number 149250.

In order to provide maximum feel for the driver, the hydraulic system did not have servo assistance, but the size of the brakes meant that emergency stops required no more pedal effort than an assisted system once the discs and pads were warm. Independent hydraulic circuits served the front and rear brakes, providing emergency braking through the second circuit should one fail; there was also a rear circuit pressure regulator. All hydraulic pipes and unions were of similar type and quality to those used in Formula 1 cars of the period.

Wheels & Tyres

As with the GTO, the F40 sat on Speedline split-rim aluminium wheels of a design unique to the model. The polished and lacquered natural-finish split rim was bolted to a silver-painted and lacquered five-spoke hub, the spokes having raised ribs on their outer edges. The wheel was mounted, competition style, on a central hub spline and secured by a single hub nut fitted with a sprung pin for security.

An emergency tyre repair/inflator canister was provided in the tool kit. Due to the car's performance potential, Ferrari recommended that a punctured tyre should be replaced, not repaired.

Wheels/Tyres

Front wheels	8Jx17
Front tyres	245/40 ZR17[1] or 235/45 ZR17[2]
Rear wheels	10Jx17
Rear tyres	335/35 ZR17[3]

[1] Size for Pirelli P Zero or Bridgestone RE71
[2] Size for Goodyear Eagle GSA or Michelin MXX
[3] All four tyre makes were the same size at the rear.

Identification Plates

The European-market F40 had identification plates and labels as follows:

1 From front to rear on the top right chassis member in the engine compartment: lubrication details plate; type approval plate; Vehicle Identification Number (VIN) plate with chassis number (see page 126 for guidance about how to decode the useful VIN information).
2 Engine type and serial number plate at the front centre of the engine block vee.
3 Chassis number and type plate in the front compartment at right-hand rear of luggage well.
4 Windscreen washer type approval label on side of reservoir in front compartment.
5 Paint label on right-hand side of front compartment in front of washer reservoir bottle.
6 Dipped beam homologation label below paint label in front compartment.
7 Tyre pressure label in driver's side bottom corner of windscreen.
8 Car type and chassis number plate in an upstand on the upper surface of the steering column.

The US version differed as follows:

1 Lubrication plate as Europe.
2 Assembly number plate in engine compartment.
3 Engine detail plate as Europe.
4 Vehicle emission control information and catalytic converter label on rear of left-hand rear inner wheel arch.
5 Vehicle emission control bar code label below 4.
6 Screen washer type approval label as Europe.
7 Chassis number plate in front compartment as Europe.
8 Paint plate as Europe.
9 No dipped beam homologation label.
10 Unleaded fuel labels in neck of filler openings.
11 Chassis number plate on steering column as Europe.
12 VIN bar code label on driver's door shut post.
13 FMV safety standard certification plate below 12.
14 Tyre pressure plate on passenger door shut post.

Plates on top right-hand chassis member in engine compartment, with, to the fore, those for type approval and Vehicle Identification Number (owner wishes to conceal last five digits, denoting chassis number).

Production Data

Model	Production period	Chassis number range	Number built
288 Evoluzione	1985-87	70167, 70205, 79887, 79888, 79889	5 (all prototypes)
F40	1987-92	76624-95317	1311 (excluding prototypes)

APPENDIX

VEHICLE IDENTIFICATION NUMBER (VIN) SYSTEM

The Vehicle Identification Number system was introduced by the Federal authorities in the USA in 1980, making it mandatory for all cars sold there to carry a 17-character identification code. Simultaneously, the European Community brought into force identical legislation for European car manufacturers, based on rules originally drawn up in 1978 under EC Directive 78/507. The VIN system – the automotive equivalent to a DNA test – provides a relatively straightforward method of determining a particular car's provenance.

Being able to read the VIN on a particular car should provide adequate information, along with the individual serial numbers, as to whether the model presented is as it originally left the factory. If there is any doubt over provenance, the Ferrari concessionaire can authenticate for any bona fide enquirer that the details provided match the specification of the car described.

The following is an explanation of the composite parts of the VIN system.

EC Directive 78/507
All VIN codes must be 17 characters, subdivided into three sections:

First section – three letters known as the WMI (World Manufacturer Identifier), which is ZFF for Ferrari or ZDF for Dino.
Second section – a mixture of six letters and numbers.
First character: letter denoting engine specification.
Second character: letter denoting the safety system.
Third and fourth characters: numbers denoting the model.
Fifth character: letter denoting the destination and variant.
Sixth character: check digit needed to comply with US and Japanese requirements.
Third section – eight characters which complete the 17.
First character: letter or number denoting model year or year of production.
Second character: number indicating the production facility.
Third to eighth characters: numbers indicating the serial number of the chassis.

A few further comments may be useful to clarify the characters used in the system.

First section
First character: always Z as this is the identity code for Italy.
Second section
First character: as there are only 26 letters available, some have been used more than once. To determine the exact type, cross-reference must be made with the third and fourth digits, which indicate model and/or body type.
Second character: eg, the letter A indicates three-point seat belts with retractor.
Third and fourth characters: eg, 03 indicates a 308 GTB, 04 a 308 GTS.
Fifth character: eg, the letter C indicates right-hand drive.
Third section
First character: eg, the letter S indicates 1995.
Second character: as all Ferraris are produced at Maranello, this is always 0.

PERFORMANCE COMPARISONS

Model	0-30mph (sec)	0-60mph (sec)	0-100mph (sec)	Top speed (mph)	Source
308 GT4 (EU)	2.5	6.9	18.0	154	A
308 GT4 (EU)	2.5	6.4	16.7	152	M
308 GT4 (US)	2.5	7.8	22.0	134	C&D
308 GT4 (US)	2.4	7.8	20.5	138	R&T
308 GTB (EU)	2.3	6.5	17.0	154	A
308 GTS (EU)	2.5	6.6	16.6	150+ (est)	T&CC
308 GTB (US)	3.1	7.9	21.1	140 (est)	C&D
308 GTB (US)	3.9	9.4	22.6	132	R&T '77
308 GTB (US)	2.3	7.3	19.8	145	R&T '80
308 GTS (US)	2.5	7.2	20.6	139	C&D
308 GTS (US)	3.5	7.3	19.8	145	R&T '78
308 GTBi (US)	2.5	7.6	22.6	140	C&D
308 GTSi (US)	2.9	7.9	22.1	140	R&T
308 GTB QV (EU)	2.1	5.7	14.3	154.5	M
308 GTS QV (US)	2.3	7.4	18.5	144	C&D
Mondial 8 (US)	3.1	9.3	27.8	138	C&D
Mondial 8 (US)	3.1	9.4	28.1	135	R&T
Mondial QV (EU)	2.2	6.4	16.2	146.1	M
Mondial QV (EU)	2.3	6.6	17.2	147.1	FL
Mondial 3.2 (EU)	2.5	6.3	15.8	148.5	M
Mondial t (EU)	2.2	5.6	13.9	154	A
328 GTB (EU)	2.1	5.5	14.2	153	A
328 GTS (US)	1.9	5.6	15.1	153	C&D
348tb (EU)	–	5.6	13.3	164	A&M
348tb (EU)	1.9	5.5	13.0	162.4	FL
348 GTS (EU)	2.6	5.9	13.9	163	A&M
288 GTO	2.0	5.0	11.0	175*	C&D
F40 (EU)	2.2	4.5	8.8	201**	A&M

*Low turbo boost pressure, factory claimed top speed 190mph
**Factory claimed top speed 201mph

Sources
PC, *Performance Car*; FL, *Fast Lane*; A&M, *Autocar & Motor*; A, *Autocar*; M, *Motor*; R&T, *Road & Track*; C&D, *Car and Driver*; T&CC, *Thoroughbred & Classic Cars*

FACTORY LITERATURE SALES/PRESS

Factory print no	Model/description	Date
87/74	308 GT4	01/74
98/74	308 GT4 (US)	01/74
–	308 GT4 single sheet (US)	01/74
98/75	308 GT4 (US)	01/75
99/76	308 GT4	01/75
101/75	208 GT4	01/75
111/75	308 GTB	08/75
119/76	308 GT4	01/76
120/76	308 GTB	02/76
120/76	308 GTB	11/76
136/77	Range folder	01/77
137/77	Range brochure	01/77
146/77	Range brochure	??/77
147/77	308 GTB/S	??/77
147/77	308 GTB/S	11/79
147/77	308 GTB/S	04/80
148/77	308 GT4	??/77
160/78	308 GT4	02/78
–	Mondial 8 press info (I)	03/80
–	Mondial 8 press info (F)	03/80
–	Mondial 8 press info (GB)	03/80
–	Mondial 8 press info (D)	03/80
182/80	Mondial 8	03/80
197/80	308 GTBi/Si (US)	07/80
199/80	Mondial 8	09/80
206/81	308 GTBi/Si	02/81
207/81	208 GTB/S single sheet	02/81
220/81	Mondial 8 (US)	09/81
225/81	308 GTBi/Si	10/81
227/81	308 GTBi/Si (US)	11/81
235/82	208 Turbo	04/82
235/82	208 Turbo	08/83
236/82	208 Turbo press info	04/82
242/82	Mondial QV (black intake)	07/82
242/82	Mondial QV (red intake)	07/82
242/82	Mondial QV (red intake)	05/83
258/83	308 QV	01/83
258/83	308 QV	03/84
272/83	308 QV (US)	04/83
284/83	Mondial QV (US)	09/83
284/83	Mondial QV (US)	01/85
296/84	Mondial Cabriolet press info, Brussels (I, F, D, GB)	01/84
296/84	Mondial Cabriolet press info, Geneva (I, F, D, GB)	02/84
305/84	288 GTO press info, Geneva (I, F, D, GB)	02/84
313/84	Mondial Cabriolet	06/84
367/85	'Eight-Cylinder' press info, Frankfurt (I, F, D, GB)	09/85
387/85	328 GTB/S	09/85
387/85	328 GTB/S	11/85
388/85	3.2 Mondial	09/85
388/85	3.2 Mondial	11/85
394/85	328 GTB/S	11/85
394/85	328 GTB/S	11/86
394/85	328 GTB/S	02/88
394/85	328 GTB/S	01/89
395/85	328 GTB/S (US)	11/85
395/85	328 GTB/S (US)	02/88
402/85	3.2 Mondial	12/85
402/85	3.2 Mondial	02/87
403/85	3.2 Mondial (US)	12/85
403/85	3.2 Mondial (Europe)	12/85
403/85	3.2 Mondial (Europe)	09/88
424/86	GTB/S Turbo press info (I)	04/86
425/86	GTB/S Turbo press info (GB)	04/86
427/86	GTB/S Turbo	04/86
443/86	GTB/S Turbo	07/86
443/87	GTB/S Turbo	10/88
–	F40 preliminary press info, white cover (I, GB, F, D)	06/87
475/87	F40 press info (I)	09/87
475/87	F40 press info (I)	06/88
476/87	F40 press info (F)	09/87
476/87	F40 press info (F)	06/88
477/87	F40 press info (GB)	09/87
477/87	F40 press info (GB)	06/88
478/87	F40 press info (D)	09/87
478/87	F40 press info (D)	06/88
479/87	F40	09/87
479/87	F40	09/88
479/87	F40	10/90
–	F40 client presentation card	??/88
504/88	Range brochure (I)	??/88

V8 Model Production at a Glance

Model	Production period	Chassis number range	Numbers built
308 GT4	1974-80	07202-15604	2826
208 GT4	1975-80	08830-15596	840
308 GTB (glass-fibre)	1975-77	18677-21289	712
308 GTB (steel)	1977-80	20805-34349	2185
308 GTS	1977-80	22619-34501	3219
Mondial 8	1980-82	31075-41727	703
208 GTB	1980-82	31219-41329	160
208 GTS	1980-82	31249-41265	140
308 GTBi	1980-82	31327-43059	494
308 GTSi	1980-82	31309-43079	1749
208 GTB Turbo	1982-85	41357-59277	437
Mondial QV Coupé	1982-85	41737-59131	1145
308 GTB QV	1982-85	42809-59071	748
308 GTS QV	1982-85	41701-59265	3042
208 GTS Turbo	1983-85	42863-59279	250
Mondial QV Cabriolet	1983-85	47247-59163	629
288 GTO	1984-86	52465-58345	272
328 GTB	1985-89	58735-83017	1344
328 GTS	1985-89	59301-83136	6068
3.2 Mondial Coupé	1985-89	58277-79671	987
3.2 Mondial Cabriolet	1985-89	59393-78895	810
GTB Turbo	1986-89	63277-83137	308
GTS Turbo	1986-89	63739-83148	828
F40	1987-92	76624-95317	1311
Mondial t	1989-93	79596-97698	858
Mondial t Cabriolet	1989-93	80339-97733	1017
348tb	1989-93	81617-96679	2894
348ts	1989-93	81651-96964	4228
348 Serie Speciale (US)	1993	92812-95820	80
348 Spider	1993-95	94504-99947	1146
348 GTB	1993-94	96655-99697	222
348 GTS	1993-94	96824-99197	218
348 GT Competizione (EU)	1993-94	96064-99143	56

V8 Production Engine Types

Model	Engine type	Description			
308GT4	F106AL	NA/C	2926cc	Wet sump	255bhp
208GT4	F106C	NA/C	1991cc	Wet sump	180bhp
308GTB/S	F106AB	NA/C	2926cc	Dry/Wet sump	255bhp
208GTB/S	F106CB	NA/C	1991cc	Wet sump	155bhp
208 Turbo	F106D	T/1	1991cc	Wet sump	220bhp
308GTBi/Si	F106BB	NA/I	2926cc	Wet sump	214bhp
Mondial 8	F106B	NA/I	2926cc	Wet sump	214bhp
308 QV	F105AB	NA/I	2926cc	Wet sump	235bhp
Mondial QV	F105A	NA/I	2926cc	Wet sump	235bhp
M. QV Cabrio	F105AS	NA/I	2926cc	Wet sump	235bhp
288GTO	F114B	T/2	2855cc	Dry sump	400bhp
328	F105CB	NA/I	3185cc	Wet sump	270bhp
3.2M. Coupé	F105C	NA/I	3185cc	Wet sump	270bhp
3.2M. Cabrio	F105CS	NA/I	3185cc	Wet sump	270bhp
GTB/S Turbo	F106N	T/1	1991cc	Wet sump	254bhp
Lancia Thema	F105L	NA/I	2927cc	Dry sump	215bhp
F40	F120A	T/2	2936cc	Dry sump	478bhp
348	F119D	NA/I	3405cc	Dry sump	300bhp
348	F119G	NA/I	3405cc	Dry sump	295bhp
348 & 348 GTC	F119H	NA/I	3405cc	Dry sump	320bhp
Mondial t	F119DL	NA/I	3405cc	Dry sump	300bhp
Mondial t	F119G	NA/I	3405cc	Dry sump	295bhp

Notes

1. All Ferrari V8 production engines have a 90° configuration, with twin overhead camshafts per bank of cylinders.
2. All figures refer to standard specification European market models.

Abbreviations

NA/C: Normally aspirated, carburettors
NA/I: Normally aspirated, fuel injection
T/1: Single turbocharger
T/2: Twin turbochargers

505/88	Range brochure (F)	??/88
506/88	Range brochure (GB)	??/88
507/888	Range brochure (D)	??/88
537/89	Range brochure	??/89
561/89	F40 (I, GB, F, D)	07/89
562/89	Mondial t	06/89
562/89	Mondial t	12/89
562/90	Mondial t	03/90
572/89	348 press info (I, GB, F, D)	09/89
573/89	Range brochures (I, GB, F, D, E)	??/89
575/89	348	10/89
575/89	348	02/90
575/89	348	05/90
575/89	348	11/90
579/89	Mondial t (I, GB, F, D)	11/89
593/90	348 (I, GB, F, D, E)	06/90
616/90	Range brochures (I, GB, F, D, E)	??/91
654/91	348 Challenge press info	10/92
720/92	Range brochure	04/92
729/92	Range brochure	05/92
788/93	348 GT	07/93
788/93	348 GT	12/93
826/94	348 GTB press folder	02/94
826/94	348 GTB press folder	04/94
827/94	348 GTS press folder	02/94
827/94	348 GTS press folder	04/94
828/94	348 Spider press folder	02/94
828/94	348 Spider press folder	04/94
828/94	348 Spider press folder	09/94
869/94	348 Spider	06/94

Where no description appears on the list, the item is a sales brochure or catalogue.

Factory Literature Parts/Repair

Factory print no	Model/description	Date
91/74	308 GT4 Owner's Handbook	05/74
94/74	308 GT4 Parts Book	07/74
95/74	308 GT4 Consumer Information (US)	09/74
100/74	308 GT4 Owner's Handbook (US)	01/75
102/75	208 GT4 Owner's Handbook	02/75
104/75	308 GT4 Workshop Manual	??/75
108/75	208 GT4 Parts Book	07/75
110/75	308 GT4 Workshop Manual (GB)	??/75
116/75	308 GTB Owner's Handbook	09/75
123/76	308 GT4 Parts Book	07/76
124/76	308 GT4 Owner's Handbook	06/76
125/76	308 GTB Consumer Information	06/77
126/76	308 GT4 Handbook Supplement (US)	01/76
127/76	308 GTB Owner's Handbook (US)	09/76
128/76	308 GTB Parts Book (US, AUS)	11/76
129/76	308 GTB Parts Book	11/76
134/76	308 GTB Owner's Handbook	10/76
135/76	308 GT4 Owner's Handbook	10/76
143/77	308 GTB Handbook Supplement (US)	01/77
144/77	308 GT4 Handbook Supplement (US)	01/77
145/77	308 GTB/S Parts Book	??/77
149/77	308 GTS Consumer Information (US)	11/77
150/78	308 GTB/S Owner's Handbook (US)	01/78
155/78	308 GTB/S Owner's Handbook	06/78
156/78	308 GT4 Handbook Supplement (US)	06/78
161/78	308 GTB/S Parts Book	01/78
163/78	308 GT4 Owner's Handbook	07/78
165/78	308 GTB/S Handbook Supplement (J)	07/78
166/78	308 GTB/S Parts Book (J)	07/78
167/79	Eight-Cylinder Time Service Schedule	01/79
172/79	308 GT4 Parts Book	03/79
184/80	308 GTBi Consumer Information (US)	03/80
185/80	308 GTSi Consumer Information (US)	03/80
186/80	308 GTBi/Si Owner's Handbook (US)	??/80
186A/80	308 GTBi/Si Owner's Handbook (US)	??/81
188/80	208 GTB/S Owner's Handbook	??/80
189/80	308 GTBi/Si Parts Book	06/80
190/80	308 GTBi/Si Owner's Handbook	??/80
191/80	Mondial 8 Owner's Handbook	??/80
193/80	308 GTBi/Si Parts Book (US)	06/80
194/80	Eight-Cylinder Time Service Schedule	05/80
195/80	308 GTBi/Si Owner's Handbook	??/80
203/81	Mondial 8 Owner's Handbook (Prov)	01/81
204/81	208 GTB/S Parts Book	01/81
205/81	Mondial 8 Parts Book	04/81
209/81	308 GTBi/Si Parts Book	01/81
210/81	Mondial 8 Consumer Information (US)	01/81
212/81	308 GTBi/Si Handbook Supplement (US)	01/81
213/81	Mondial 8 Time Service Schedule	06/81
214/81	Mondial 8 Parts Book (US)	09/81
215/81	Mondial 8 Owner's Manual (US)	??/81

216/81	308 GTBi/Si Owner's Manual (US)	??/81
216/81	Mondial 8 Owner's Manual (US)	??/81
222/81	308 GTBi/Si Parts Book (US)	??/81
223/81	Mondial 8 Wiring Diagrams	??/81
231/82	208 Turbo Parts Book	06/82
239/82	208 Turbo Owner's Handbook	??/82
–	Mondial QV Parts Book	09/82
–	Mondial QV Owner's Handbook	??/82
241/82	Mondial QV Owner's Handbook	??/82
259/83	308 QV Parts Book (US)	??/83
260/83	308 QV Owner's Handbook (US)	??/83
261/83	308 GTS QBV Consumer Information (US)	??/83
262/83	308 GTB QV Consumer Information (US)	??/83
263/83	Mondial QV Consumer Information (US)	??/83
264/83	Mondial QV Parts Book (US)	??/83
265/83	Mondial QV Owner's Handbook (US)	??/83
267/83	308 QV 'Safety & Safety' booklet	02/83
273/83	308 QV Wiring Diagrams (US)	05/83
274/83	208 Turbo Time Service Schedule	04/83
275/83	Mondial QV Time Service Schedule	04/83
275/83	Mondial QV Time Service Schedule	05/83
276/83	308 QV Time Service Schedule	06/83
280/83	Mondial Cabrio Consumer Information (US)	??/83
281/83	Mondial QV Workshop Manual	??/83
282/83	Mondial QV Air Conditioning Info	??/83
285/83	Mondial QV Handbook Supplement (CH)	??/83
286/83	308 QV Handbook Supplement (CH)	??/83
289/83	Mondial QV Wiring Diagrams (US)	??/83
290/83	Mondial Cabrio Add' Instructions (US)	??/83
293/83	Mondial QV Time Service Schedule	12/83
300/85	Mondial Cabrio Handbook Supplement (US)	??/84
302/84	308 QV Parts Book (US)	03/84
303/84	308 QV Wiring Diagrams	??/84
307/84	308 QV Owner's Handbook (US)	03/84
308/84	Mondial QV Owner's Handbook (US)	04/84
309/84	Mondial Cabrio Handbook Supplement (US)	04/84
310/84	Mondial QV Add' Parts Book (US)	04/84
311/84	Mondial QV Parts Book	05/84
312/84	Mondial QV Time Service Schedule	05/84
314/84	308 QV Wiring Diagrams (US)	??/84
317/84	Mondial Cabrio Wiring Diagrams (US)	09/84
318/84	Mondial QV Owner's Handbook (AUS)	??/84
331/84	288 GTO Parts Book	12/84
341/85	208 Turbo Lubrication Chart	??/85
342/85	208 QV Lubrication Chart	??/85
343/85	Mondial QV Lubrication Chart	??/85
345/85	288 GTO Owner's Handbook	??/85
350/85	288 GTO Time Service Schedule	??/85
–	288 GTO Injection/Ignition Handbook	??/85
361/85	308 QV Parts Book	??/85
372/85	328 GTB/S Consumer Information (US)	??/85
373/85	3.2 Mondial Consumer Information (US)	??/85
374/85	328 Parts Book	??/85
375/85	3.2 Mondial Parts Book	??/85
376/85	328 Owner's Handbook	??/85
376/86	328 Owner's Handbook	??/86
377/85	3.2 Mondial Owners Handbook	??/85
379/85	288 Gearbox/Differential Manual	??/85
389/85	328 GTB/S Temp' Instruction Book	??/85
390/85	3.2 Mondial Temp' Instruction Book	??/85
391/85	288 GTO Diagnosis with IAW Tester	??/85
396/85	328 Owner's Handbook (US)	??/85
397/85	3.2 Mondial Owner's Handbook (US)	??/85
404/85	328 Time Service Schedule	??/85
405/85	3.2 Mondial Time Service Schedule	??/85
414/86	328 Consumer Information (US)	??/86
415/86	3.2 Mondial Consumer Information (US)	??/86
419/86	3.2 Mondial Wiring Diagrams	??/86
428/86	GTB/S Turbo Provisional Handbook	??/86
429/86	GTB/S Turbo Owner's Handbook	??/86
432/86	GTB/S Turbo Parts Book	??/86
433/86	GTB/S Turbo Time Service Schedule	??/86
434/87	328 Owner's Handbook Supplement (CH)	??/86
435/86	3.2 Mondial Owner's Handbook Supplement (CH)	??/86
438.86	328 Wiring Diagram	??/86
439/96	GTB/S Turbo Wiring Diagram	??/86
440/86	328 Wiring Diagram	??/86
442/86	3.2 Mondial Wiring Diagram	??/86
442/87	3.2 Mondial Wiring Diagram	11/87
458/86	328 Owner's Handbook (US)	??/86
462/87	328 Parts Book	??/87
473/87	3.2 Mondial Parts Book	??/87
474/87	3.2 Mondial Owner's Handbook	??/87
481/87	3.2 Mondial Owner's Handbook (US)	??/87
481/87	328 Owner's Handbook (US)	??/87
486/87	3.2 Mondial Consumer Info (US)	??/87
487/87	3.2 Mondial Owner's Handbook	??/87
488/87	3.2 Mondial Wiring Diagram	??/87
489/87	3.2 Mondial Wiring Diagram (US)	??/87
493/88	328 Owner's Handbook	??/88
494/88	GTB/S Turbo Owner's Handbook	??/88
497/88	3.2 Mondial Owner's Handbook	??/88
512A/88	F40 Owner's Handbook	??/88
513/88	328 Owner's Handbook	09/88
516/88	F40 Temporary Parts Book	04/88
517/88	3.2 Mondial Owner's Handbook (CH)	07/88
518/88	328 Owner's Handbook (CH, A, S)	??/88
521/88	F40 Parts Book	10/88
522/88	328 ABS Brakes Manual	??/88
524/88	328 Parts Book	??/88
530/88	328 Consumer Information (US)	??/88
530/89	328 Consumer Information (US)	??/89
534/88	Eight-Cylinder ABS Brakes Manual	??/88
535/88	328 Owner's Handbook (US)	01/89
539/89	Bosch KE3 Jetronic Manual	??/89
548/89	GTB/S Turbo Parts Book	05/89
550/89	308 QV/328 Workshop Manual	??/89
551/89	GTB/S Turbo Owner's Handbook	??/89
553/89	Mondial t Owner's Handbook	??/89
554/89	F40 Workshop Manual	??/89
554/89	F40 Workshop Manual	10/90
559/89	328 Wiring Diagram	??/89
563/89	V8 Time Service Schedule	??/89
564/89	348 Owner's Handbook	??/89
–	348 Temporary Parts Book	??/89
567/89	Mondial t Consumer Information (US)	??/89
568/89	348 Consumer Information (US)	??/89
570/89	Mondial t Owner's Handbook (US)	??/89
571/89	348 Owner's Handbook (US)	??/89
594/90	F40 Consumer Information (US)	??/90
595/90	348 Owner's Handbook	??/90
596/90	Mondial t Owner's Handbook	??/90
600/90	348/Mondial t Consumer Information	??/90
601/90	348 Consumer Information (US)	??/90
604/90	348 Workshop Manual	??/90
606/90	F40 Owner's Handbook (US)	??/90
610/90	F40 Catalyser Manual	??/90
611/90	348 Parts Book	??/90
613/90	348 Owner's Handbook (US)	??/90
624/90	Mondial t Workshop Manual	11/90
625/90	348 Gearbox/Clutch Manual	12/90
627/90	F40 Time Service Schedule	12/90
629/90	Mondial t Owner's Handbook (US)	??/90
630/90	F40 Catalyser Manual	12/90
635/90	348 Owner's Handbook (US)	10/90
642/91	348 Owner's Handbook	01/91
642/91	348 Owner's Handbook	06/91
643/91	V8 Time Service Schedule	02/91
646/91	Mondial t Workshop Manual	??/91
647/91	F40 Workshop Manual	??/91
649/91	Mondial t Owner's Handbook	??/91
650/91	F40 Parts Book	??/91
651/91	Mondial t Workshop Manual	??/91
652/91	348 Workshop Manual	??/91
653/91	Mondial t Gearbox/Clutch Manual	06/91
658/91	348 Owner's Handbook (US)	07/91
659/91	Mondial t Owner's Handbook (US)	10/91
660/91	F40 Owner's Handbook (US)	07/91
705/92	348 Owner's Handbook	??/92
709/92	Mondial t Workshop Manual (US)	03/92
710/92	348 Workshop Manual (US)	03/92
728/92	348 Owner's Handbook	06/92
737/92	Mondial t Owner's Handbook	10/82
739/92	348 Consumer Information (US)	09/92
754/92	Mondial t Mechanical Parts Book	11/92
764/93	Mondial t Parts Book	02/93
777/93	Mondial t Valeo Manual	??/93
770/93	348 Consumer Information (US)	??/93
775/93	348 Spider Owner's Handbook (US)	05/93
776/93	348 Lubrication Chart	04/93
779/93	348 Owner's Handbook	04/93
780/93	Valeo Clutch Manual	05/93
781/93	348 Challenge Kit Manual	05/93
782/93	348 Parts Catalogue	05/93
787/93	348 Spider Owner's Handbook	??/93
798/93	348 Spider Workshop Manual Section L	07/93
801/93	348 GT Owner's Handbook	09/93
811/93	348 GT '94 Model Year Owner's Handbook	??/94
823/94	348 GT Competizione Handbook Supplement	03/94
834/94	348 Challenge '94 Regulations	03/94
837/94	348 '94 Parts Book	04/94
839/94	348 Spider Owner's Handbook (US)	04/94
920/94	348 GT Competizione W/shop Manual	??/95
939/95	'95 Challenge Regulations	02/95
943/95	'95 348 Challenge Manual	02/95

FACTORY POSTERS

Factory print no	Model/description	Date
121/76	308 GTB	02/76
153/78	308 GTS	01/78
154/78	308 GT4	01/78
233/82	Mondial 8	??/82
237/82	208 Turbo	??/82
319/84	288 GTO	08/84
319/84	288 GTO	02/85
320/84	288 GTO	08/84
320/84	288 GTO	02/85
380/85	328 GTS Drawing	09/85
381/85	3.2 Mondial Drawing	09/85
382/85	3.2 Mondial Cabriolet Drawing	09/85
386/85	3.2 Engine Drawing	09/85
398/85	328	11/85
398/85	328	02/87
398/85	328	09/88
399/85	3.2 Mondial	11/85
399/85	3.2 Mondial	02/87
416/86	328 GTS	03/86
444/86	GTB Turbo	07/86
490/87	F40	10/87
490/87	F40	06/88
491/87	F40	10/87
491/87	F40	06/88
492/87	F40	10/87
492/87	F40	06/88
532/88	F40	12/88
533/89	F40	11/89
533/90	F40	03/90
533/90	F40	11/90
576/89	F40	??/89
589/90	348tb	05/90
590/90	348tb	05/90
591/90	348tb	05/90
592/90	348ts	05/90
617/90	348tb	11/90
618/90	348ts	11/90
619/90	Mondial t	11/90
620/90	Mondial t Cabriolet	11/90
622/90	F40	11/90
761/93	348 Spider	??/93
763/93	348 Spider	03/93